Praise for *Invest by Knowing What Stocks to Buy and What Stocks to Sell*

"This is one of the best new investing books of the decade: succinct, practical, and timeless. Built on a foundation of 40 years of market wisdom, it combines technical analysis and portfolio construction that is supported by excellent research. It should be required reading for everyone from new investors to the most sophisticated hedge fund managers."

—Linda Raschke, President, LBRGroup, Inc.

"The author is an award winning Technical Analyst. In this book, he covers the basic principles, definitions, safeguards, pitfalls, and risks of investing. Believing in active management, he recognizes the benefits of multiple tools (fundamental and technical) and disciplines there-on, to construct a portfolio methodology with guidelines for both buying and selling, for maximum gain. This is a valuable book for any serious investor."

—Louise Yamada, Managing Director, Louise Yamada Technical Research Advisors, LLC.

"In this book, Charles Kirkpatrick demonstrates just how powerful a tool relative strength is, deftly combining technical and fundamental analysis to produce a superior long-term approach. This isn't just theory, but the real-time work of a practitioner with an outstanding track record. For many years a small group of knowledgeable investors has known about this work, now you can too."

—John Bollinger, CFA, CMT, President, Bollinger Capital Management

"The author presents a clearly written, time-tested formula for investor independence and success through applying relative price strength for stock selection and portfolio construction."

—Hank Pruden, Golden Gate University

**BEAT
THE
MARKET**

**INVEST BY KNOWING
WHAT STOCKS
TO BUY AND WHAT
STOCKS TO SELL**

BEAT THE MARKET

INVEST BY KNOWING WHAT STOCKS TO BUY AND WHAT STOCKS TO SELL

CHARLES D. KIRKPATRICK II, CMT

Vice President, Publisher: Tim Moore
Associate Publisher and Director of Marketing: Amy Neidlinger
Executive Editor: Jim Boyd
Editorial Assistant: Heather Luciano
Development Editor: Russ Hall
Operations Manager: Gina Kanouse
Digital Marketing Manager: Julie Phifer
Publicity Manager: Laura Czaja
Assistant Marketing Manager: Megan Colvin
Marketing Assistant: Brandon Smith
Cover Designer: R&D&Co
Managing Editor: Kristy Hart
Project Editor: Chelsey Marti
Copy Editor: Deadline Driven Publishing
Proofreader: Paula Lowe
Indexer: Erika Millen
Compositor: Nonie Ratcliff
Manufacturing Buyer: Dan Uhrig

© 2009 by Pearson Education, Inc.
Publishing as FT Press
Upper Saddle River, New Jersey 07458

This book is sold with the understanding that neither the author nor the publisher is engaged in rendering legal, accounting or other professional services or advice by publishing this book. Each individual situation is unique. Thus, if legal or financial advice or other expert assistance is required in a specific situation, the services of a competent professional should be sought to ensure that the situation has been evaluated carefully and appropriately. The author and the publisher disclaim any liability, loss, or risk resulting directly or indirectly, from the use or application of any of the contents of this book.

FT Press offers excellent discounts on this book when ordered in quantity for bulk purchases or special sales. For more information, please contact U.S. Corporate and Government Sales, 1-800-382-3419, corpsales@pearsontechgroup.com. For sales outside the U.S., please contact International Sales at international@pearson.com.

Company and product names mentioned herein are the trademarks or registered trademarks of their respective owners.

All rights reserved. No part of this book may be reproduced, in any form or by any means, without permission in writing from the publisher.

Printed in the United States of America

Second Printing October 2008

ISBN-10: 0-13-243978-6
ISBN-13: 978-0-13-243978-7

Pearson Education LTD.
Pearson Education Australia PTY, Limited.
Pearson Education Singapore, Pte. Ltd.
Pearson Education North Asia, Ltd.
Pearson Education Canada, Ltd.
Pearson Educatión de Mexico, S.A. de C.V.
Pearson Education—Japan
Pearson Education Malaysia, Pte. Ltd.

Kirkpatrick, Charles D.
  Beat the market / Charles D. Kirkpatrick, II.
    p. cm.
  Includes bibliographical references.
  ISBN 0-13-243978-6 (hardback : alk. paper) 1. Portfolio management. 2. Investment analysis. 3. Stocks. 4. Investments. I. Title.
  HG4529.5.K565 2009
  332.6—dc22
                        2008014970

To Robert A. Levy, a relative pioneer

Contents

Introduction 1

CHAPTER 1   **Investing Today** 3
                  Investment Management 4
                  Investment Management Incentive 5
                  What Do You Do? 15
                  Summary 18

CHAPTER 2   **Beliefs and Biases** 19
                  The Markets 20
                  My Emotional Experience 22
                  Summary 25

CHAPTER 3   **Investment Risk** 27
                  Individual Stock Risk 27
                  Randomness 29
                  Diversification 30
                  Law of Percentages 31
                  Drawdown 31
                  Market Risk 33
                  Summary 37

CHAPTER 4   **Conventional Analysis** 39
                  Fundamental Versus Technical Methods 39
                  Summary 46

CHAPTER 5	**Prediction Versus Reaction** 47
	Economists 47
	Gurus and "Experts" 49
	Mutual Funds 50
	Security Analysts 50
	Reaction Technique 53
	Summary 55
CHAPTER 6	**Meeting the Relatives** 57
	Value 58
	Growth 61
	Price Strength 63
	The Evidence 67
	Summary 68
CHAPTER 7	**Value Selection** 69
	Performance Three Months Ahead 73
	Performance Six Months Ahead 74
	Performance Twelve Months Ahead 77
	Advancing and Declining Background Market 78
	Relative Price-to-Sales Percentile During a Declining Market After Three Months 81
	Summary 83
CHAPTER 8	**Relative Reported EarningsGrowth Selection** .. 85
	Summary 93
CHAPTER 9	**Relative Price Strength Selection** 95
	Relative Strength Calculations 95
	Summary 105
CHAPTER 10	**Putting It Together** 109
	Growth Model 109
	Value Model 113

	Summary of Growth and Value List Triggers	116
	New Model (Called the "Bargain List")	118
	Summary	122
CHAPTER 11	**Selecting and Deleting Stocks**	**125**
	Buying	125
	Selling	127
	Sources of Relative Information	130
	Other Concerns	131
	How to Act	132
	Summary	135
CHAPTER 12	**Creating a Portfolio of Stocks**	**137**
	Maximum Drawdown	138
	Simple but Practical Methods of Creating a Portfolio	138
	Summary	146
	Conclusion	147
APPENDIX	**Investment Procedure Example**	**149**
	Finding Data, Calculating Data, and Locating Sources	149
	The Hypothetical Value Model Portfolio	150
	Performance of Value Model	152
	Adding and Deleting Stocks	154
	References	**157**
	Index	**159**

ACKNOWLEDGMENTS

In this business you come across many people who help you in ways large and small. They are people not in the investment business and they are people familiar with some of the most complicated and intricate investment methods available. I learn from them all. To name them is impossible.

This book is the result of almost 30 years of intermittent research. I began with Bob Levy to whom this book is dedicated, and I will not stop until my end. In between, there have been numerous portfolio managers, analysts, traders, professors, software designers, statisticians, students, and just plain practical investors. I refer to a few, but not to the exclusion of the many who have helped, sometimes in unknown ways.

In a series of talks on the subject of "relatives" over the past several years I have spoken at the University of Colorado, Howard University, the University of Texas (San Antonio), St. Mary's University, and MIT. To all those professors and students who criticized, suggested changes, and commented on the study, I thank you for your help. To those attending my lectures sponsored by the Market Technicians Association and the American Association of Professional Technical Analysts, I thank you for your interest and suggestions.

Several individuals reviewed earlier manuscripts of this book. They are Dick Arms, Julie Dahlquist, Mike Kahn, Mike Moody, Michael Tomsett, and Leo Trudel. Remember that I am responsible for any foolish errors or slip-ups. They were kind enough to spend considerable time reviewing and adjusting without the added burden of responsibility for mistakes. I thank them profusely for their effort.

To the FT Press people—Jim Boyd, Chelsey Marti, and Ginny Munroe—and of course all those others who performed behind the scenes and who are but shadows to me, I thank you all for making the publishing process so smooth and complete.

About this time in acknowledgements most of the thanks have been given. There is no superlative, however, that can be used to describe my appreciation of the time, anguish, missed dinners, canceled trips, and late nights suffered by my wife, Ellie, over the past two years. I would truly be lost without her.

About the Author

Charles D. Kirkpatrick II, CMT is currently president of Kirkpatrick & Company, Inc., Kittery, Maine. This is a private corporation specializing in technical research that publishes the *Kirkpatrick Market Strategist* advisory newsletter.

In the recent past, Mr. Kirkpatrick has been a director of the Market Technicians Association—an association of professional analysts—and served on its Dow Award Committee, Education Committee, and as chairman of the Academic Liaison Committee. He was editor of the *Journal of Technical Analysis*—the official journal of technical analysis research—and an instructor in finance at the Fort Lewis College School of Business Administration in Durango, Colorado—one of only seven colleges (as opposed to universities) in the U.S. accredited by the Association to Advance Collegiate Schools of Business (AACSB). In 2007, with co-author, Professor Julie Dahlquist, he published a textbook on technical analysis: *Technical Analysis—The Complete Resource for Financial Market Technicians*—now used in university finance classes and the Market Technicians Association's professional education programs.

In addition, Mr. Kirkpatrick has received awards from his peers. In 1993 and 2001 he received the Charles H. Dow Award—for excellence in technical research—and in 2008, he received the Market Technicians Association Annual Award—an award given once a year to someone for "Outstanding

Contributions to the Field of Technical Analysis." He is a graduate of Phillips Exeter Academy, Harvard College, and the Wharton School of the University of Pennsylvania, and served as a decorated combat officer in the First Cavalry Division in Vietnam. He currently resides on an island in Maine with his wife, Ellie, and various domestic animals.

Introduction

If you manage your own investments and want to understand what investing methods are worthwhile and what methods are best avoided, this book is for you. It is also for those who wish to manage their own investments but don't know how to do it. You will understand the problems and costs of professional management and the inconsistencies in traditional investment methods. You will explore three methods using different information to buy and to sell stocks. Most books on investment leave out what to do after you have bought stocks. I show you when they should be sold. The historic results of these methods, when melded together, have proven reliable in all kinds of markets over the past 30 years. I show you that the stock market is still the best investment vehicle, how and when to buy and sell individual stocks, when to be out of the market, and how to construct a working portfolio. Above all, I show you that it is impossible to predict markets or the economy, but it is still probable that you can make money. You must react to circumstances rather than predict outcomes. Using these methods, you will find that you can successfully invest for yourself.

My purpose is to show how you, by yourself, can outperform the stock market and reduce the risk of capital loss from poor decisions. You do not need to pay outrageous fees or be subjected to the incomprehensible and often incorrect theories or deceptive jargon that is thrown at you by brokers and money managers trying to get your money under their management. However, if you prefer to use advisors in the allocation of your assets, please be critical of their past performance, the reasons and history of their advice, and the fee structure and hidden costs not only of your advisor, but also of the investments in which your assets are placed. These fees can act as a significant deterrent to your portfolio's performance.

The opinions contained in this book are from my 40 years experience as a research analyst, portfolio manager, stock market newsletter writer, block desk trader, institutional broker, technical analyst, and hedge fund manager. I have owned a brokerage firm and passed at one time or another the requirements for investment advisor, options specialist, registered representative, and options and financial principal. I am the coauthor of *Technical Analysis: The Complete Reference for Financial Market Technicians*, which is used in many colleges and universities for their investment courses and has become the primary textbook for the Certified Market Technician (CMT) designation by the Market Technicians Association. I am past editor of the *Journal of Technical Analysis* and a past board member of both the Market Technicians Association and the Market Technicians Association Educational Foundation. In addition, I am the only person (so far) to have twice won the annual Charles H. Dow award for research. In short, I have been around the financial and investment markets for a long time, and I have been exposed to just about every technique, method, theory, and sales pitch put forth in the past 40 years. My father was one of the most successful portfolio managers at Fidelity before Peter Lynch. I began the "game" when I was 14, occasionally working for him in following stocks for his trust accounts. I also graduated from Harvard (AB) and the Wharton School (MBA).

Chapter 1

Investing Today

Investment management today has slowly migrated away from the old trust and prudent man concept when an experienced investment manager or trust officer looked after you, your family's investments, and your financial future. As an investor, you have to make decisions affecting your retirement and economic well-being for many reasons. Fear of litigation for poor past performance and the sheer size and complexity of investments have caused the investment industry to consolidate into specialists rather than generalists. As an example, pension funds have changed from "defined benefit" plans, where the pension fund made the investment decisions and guaranteed you a specific income after retirement, to "defined contribution" plans, where you must make your own investment decisions and hope for the best. This change takes the investment responsibility away from the pension fund and places it on you, even while you continue to pay for the "expertise" the fund allegedly offers. Now you must decide how many bonds and stocks to include in your investment program. You must decide whether to own big caps, foreign stocks, midsized, emerging market stocks, and so forth. Not being a professional, you face a daunting task. Even funds that balance investments between cash, bonds, and stocks are rare today because they are not "sexy" and have almost never outperformed the stock market.

This is unfortunate because the money management business has little incentive to watch out for you and take responsibility for your assets. In many ways, it has become a flim-flam, principally designed to take your money through fees and commissions while appearing to be on your side.

Investment Management

Let's face it, professional money management, on average, is not that great. In fact, it is a disgrace. History shows that the performance of most mutual funds is below that of the market averages. In a study by Motley Fool, from 1963 through 1998 (good years in the stock market), the average mutual fund earned for the investor approximately 2 percent less than the average market return. The study equates this to an investor earning 8 percent per year from professional management versus 10 percent per year from just buying a market average such as the Dow Jones Industrial Index (unadjusted for inflation). Using these figures, over 50 years, $10,000 invested would amount to a total market worth of $1,170,000. However, at 8 percent, the investor would have gained only $470,000. Motley Fool quotes John Bogle, founder of the Vanguard funds:

> "Our hypothetical fund investor has earned $1,170,000, donated $700,000 to the mutual fund industry, and kept the remaining $470,000. The financial system has consumed 60 percent of the return, the fund investor has achieved but 40 percent of his earnings potential. Yet, it

was the investor who provided 100 percent of the initial capital; the industry provided none. Confronted by the issue in this way, would an intelligent investor consider this split to represent a fair shake?"

With these profits, you can see why the mutual fund industry wants your money.

In the investment industry, there is almost no consideration for getting out of stocks during bear markets, and the popular policy of "diversification" (also called "asset allocation") shows meager results over long periods. In other words, it is mere gimmick with no real substance. The one thing professional management is good at is scaring many people into not investing for themselves and placing their financial assets with management. This is done primarily through investment jargon that makes the subject appear much more complicated than it is. Amazingly, this use of special words and concepts of finance theory intimidates even the higher-ups in corporations, foundations, and the wealthy who are looking for people to invest their funds. I show you that so-called finance theory has enormous logical holes in it, and in fact, it is unable to be used profitably in investing. It is a theory that has not worked well in practice but is useful in bamboozling prospective clients.

Investment Management Incentive

Investment management is not necessarily looking for the same performance of your assets as you are. It is looking at your assets as a business in which it can prosper regardless of whether you make money. Depending on the type of management, this profit incentive can work against you.

Mutual Funds and Professional Management

At one time, in the '50s and '60s, when giants such as Dreyfus and Fidelity were rapidly growing, the incentive to attract assets, as with hedge funds today, was the performance of the fund. It was this background that generated the Peter Lynches and Gerry Tsais who had high-profile performance far outstripping the market averages. However, these managers were few in number, and when other funds attempted to compete, they could not find managers who could perform much better than the market. At that point, different methods of sales and marketing developed. Fidelity and other fund management companies, for example, spent money on advertising and formed new funds every year to soak up the money intended for each investment fad. Different industry groups or themes come and go as "hot" industries in the markets. For example, if airline stocks are strong, people generally want to buy airlines. Fund management formed an airline fund to soak up that demand. Never mind that when the public finally recognized that a new trend was in process, it was near the end of the trend instead of at the beginning. To fund managers, the industry fad was irrelevant. To them, the money (your money) was captured and paying a fee. Later, when a new industry fad roared, your funds easily could be switched to another newly created fund, and the fees derived from this captive money would continue to flow to fund management.

When brokerage commissions declined, other mutual fund management companies developed close relationships with stockbrokers, who, for a portion of the trading commissions (until they became too small) and a portion of the sales fees, would push the funds to their clients. To some extent, this method still exists today. When the SEC discouraged these kickbacks, the brokerage firms and banks began their own in-house funds and pushed their clients into them, capturing both the management fees and brokerage commissions. However, neither the fad fund nor the brokerage sales methods were, or are, beneficial to the interests of the client. Indeed, they almost guarantee that the client's investments will fall behind in performance because of the high costs and poor management. In Table 1.1, I show the possible fees you may pay for the privilege of owning a mutual fund. Not all funds have all the fees outlined in the table.

TABLE 1.1 MUTUAL FUND FEES
(source: www.sec.gov/amswers/mffees.htm)

Mutual Fund Fee	Brief Description
Sales loads, including Sales Charge (load) on purchases and Deferred Sales Charge	Brokerage sales charges come in two forms: 1. a charge when you buy the fund (front-end sales load) or 2. a charge when you redeem the fund (back-end sales load). The front-end load means you have less of your money invested in the beginning. The fund must perform well before your investment is even. This is limited to 8.5 percent.
Redemption fee	Fee paid to compensate the mutual fund for costs associated with the redemption. This is limited to 2 percent.
Exchange fee	Fee paid for transferring to another fund under the same management.
Account fee	Fee paid for maintenance of an account.
Purchase fee	Fee paid for purchasing shares that goes directly to the fund, not a broker.
Management fee	Fee paid for management of the fund.

(continues)

TABLE 1.1   CONTINUED

Mutual Fund Fee	Brief Description
Distribution (12b-1) fees	Fee paid for distribution expenses and shareholder service expenses. Distribution fee includes marketing and selling fund shares (using your money to raise more money for management) and is limited to 0.75 percent. Shareholder service fee for responding to questions by shareholders and is limited to 0.25 percent. (In 1997, $9.5 billion in these fees paid by mutual fund invesors.)
Other expenses	Expenses not included in management or distribution fees, such as custodial, legal, accounting, transfer agent, and other administrative expenses.

Most investors do not consider the motives of money management firms competing for their accounts. In the past, for example, stockbrokers made their income from commissions on trades. Performance was not as important to them as the number of buys and sells they could generate. It was called "churning," which is a terrible (though profitable) incentive that encouraged high turnover in accounts and worked directly against the interests of the client because commission fees were high. Today, these commission rates have been reduced to extremely low levels and are no longer a major concern to investors. To combat this decline in income from commissions, stockbrokers have joined with the mutual fund industry (directly or indirectly) and are now interested in how much of your assets they can gather under their management. Their economic incentive is the management fee, wrap fee, or 12b(1) fee. John Bogle, in a 2003 interview with Motley Fool, said:

> "It [the mutual fund industry] has a profound conflict of interest between the managers who run the funds and the shareholders who own them ... Management fees in this

industry run about 1.6 percent for the average equity fund. By the time you add in portfolio turnover costs, which nobody discloses, the impact of sales charges and opportunity costs because funds aren't fully invested, and the out-of-pocket fees, you are probably talking about another 1.4 percent of cost, bringing that 1.6 percent management fee or expense ratio up to 3 percent a year. That is an awful lot of money."

At least in the old days, brokers had to know something about the markets. Today, the markets are almost irrelevant to them. A broker is more interested in getting your money under house management and collecting his percentage of the management fees; and, by no small coincidence, the types and names of the fee charges are staggering and complex. A broker doesn't need to know about markets, just as a car salesman doesn't need to know the intricacies of an engine, but a broker does need to know about financial jargon to impress you with his "special knowledge." As a test at your favorite brokerage office, ask how many of the brokers receive the *Barron's Financial* and actually read it. You will be surprised at how few modern brokers closely follow the market. It is unconscionable that brokers generally have separated themselves from direct contact with the markets and are now so closely involved in selling investment management by others.

The incentive of payment for gathering assets under management is also not in the best interest of the client. Fees have tripled since the late 1960s. When I began in the business in 1966, ½ of 1 percent of stock assets and ¹⁄₄₀ of 1 percent of bond assets were the standard fees. Compare those fees with the 2 percent or higher fees of today when performance has not improved at all. In addition, these fees are unrelated to the success of the client's asset growth. They are flat fees, paid regardless of whether your investment in the fund rises or falls. The fund can perform poorly, but as long as new assets are added to the fund pool, the fund management profits despite the performance for the individual client. Today, the definition of "broker" is what you will be when these modern-day experts are done with you.

The management of your investments only on a fee basis is not necessarily in line with your objectives. You pay the fee whether you profit or lose. There is no incentive for the manager under such an arrangement to perform better than the markets. He is paid no matter what happens. The better fee arrangement is when your manager profits when you do and doesn't profit when your investments fall behind. In this arrangement, you and the manager are on the same side and your fortunes should coincide. Unfortunately for you, but fortunately for the investment management business, the Investment Act of 1940 prohibits this arrangement. When challenges to the act are raised, the mutual fund industry fights vehemently against them. Quite obviously, they prefer the current arrangement of profiting despite your success or failure.

Hedge Funds

The hedge fund industry began as a way of avoiding the 1940 Act. Hedge funds enable the manager to participate in profits and to use investment methods, such as short selling, that are otherwise prohibited. A hedge fund is simply a partnership arrangement between limited partners, the investors whose legal risks are limited, and the general partners (the managers who profit above the investors when the fund does well). The partnership avoids the restrictions of the 1940 Act by operating outside of it. The hedge fund industry has grown considerably since the days of the original fund created by A. W. Jones who used the classic hedge fund formula that bought strong stocks and sold short weak ones.

DEFINITIONS

Buy long is to pay cash and purchase stock. You are then long on the stock because you own it. You make a profit when you sell it at a price higher than what you paid for it. *Sell short* is to sell stock that you have borrowed from someone else. You or your broker borrow the stock, sell it in the marketplace, and wait for its price to decline. You are then short the stock. Eventually, you must buy it back (a *short squeeze* is when many people have to buy it back because the price suddenly goes up). You buy it back in the marketplace and return it to the lender. Your intention is to sell it first at a high price and buy it back later at a low price, making a profit.

DEFINITIONS

A *hedge* is when you enter a position and enter another position in an investment that will act opposite from your original position. It is like an insurance policy in that it protects your original position from substantial loss. For example, *hedge funds* buy strong stocks and hedge them by selling short, weak stocks. By doing this, they avoid or reduce market risk. Because the longs and the shorts tend to rise and fall with the market, in a rising market, the fund profits from the long positions and suffers from the short positions. Just the opposite occurs during a declining market. The market action on the portfolio is reduced, and profits come from the correct decisions on the stock positions alone.

Definitions

A *basket of stocks* is a portfolio of stocks. Sometimes the portfolio has a theme, such as a gold basket holding only gold stocks or an airline basket holding airline stocks. The basket can be any size and have any number of stocks. When an institutional customer sells a number of stocks at one time, a brokerage firm may bid for the entire basket. It then can sell each stock individually.

Definitions

Margin refers to when an investor borrows money to purchase or sell short stock. The Federal Reserve and the exchanges regulate the amount of money you can borrow on a stock position depending on many factors. When you have purchased more stock than what you can pay for and have borrowed to make up the difference, you are said to be *on margin*.

Definitions

Derivatives are tradable contracts that by themselves have no value, but instead, they depend on their underlying investment for price action. The most common derivatives are options and futures. They have no real value because they are only contracts to buy or sell an underlying stock, commodity, or basket. For example, when you buy a Standard & Poor 500 (S&P 500) futures contract, you promise to pay the amount that the Standard & Poor index (S&P index) is worth (multiplied by some factor) on the day that the contract expires. The price of the future, therefore, oscillates with the price of the S&P index until it expires, but without the S&P 500, it is worthless.

The name "hedge fund" has remained for most investment partnerships, regardless of their investment style or methods. Because the incentive of participation in profits is attractive to investment managers, and was especially during the great bull market of the 1990s, many managers quit the mutual fund industry and began their own funds. They wanted to profit from their decisions rather than receive just a salary and perhaps a year-end bonus. Unfortunately, the Securities & Exchange Commission (SEC) impose limits on the amount of money an individual can invest in these funds, usually a million dollars, putting such investments out of the reach of most people.

There are developing problems in the hedge fund industry as well. Fees are still very high, often 2 percent of assets invested in the fund plus 20 percent of the profits. In addition, because the fees are so attractive to investment managers, the industry has attracted some less-than-scrupulous people. Finally, the market no longer rises every day as it did in the 1990s and easy money is no longer available. Indeed, average hedge fund performance over the past five years is only slightly better than that of the stock market. This means that fund managers will take larger risks with your invested money because they want more than the fixed fee. Generally, they risk the assets of the fund with leverage (borrowed money, sometimes as much as 200 to 1,—that is for every dollar invested they borrow $200) and open themselves to the risk of failure. If they fail, you lose, and they generally walk away.

ETFs (Exchange Traded Fund)

In recent years, tradable securities called ETFs (Exchange Traded Fund) have been introduced to replicate the action of stocks in a known or associated basket. The securities or commodities in the basket are known to the ETF buyer, and unlike mutual funds, they remain in the portfolio. ETFs can be bought long, sold short, margined, and may even have tradable options and futures. Standard orders, such as market, stop loss, and limit, may be used that are not available for mutual funds. They are priced immediately in the marketplace, not periodically as in mutual funds, and there is no minimum investment required. The components of each ETF follow themes as different and diverse as the Brazilian stock market, high growth stocks, the S&P 500, utilities indices, commodities such as gold or petroleum, and even municipal bonds. The number of possible themes is limitless; thus, these instruments have been introduced at a speedy rate. The costs of ownership are less than mutual funds because there are no high-priced managers (the portfolio is run by a computer). ETF operating costs are usually between 0.1 percent and 1.0 percent. They are generally easy to buy and sell because they are listed on exchanges and Nasdaq, and brokerage costs to trade them are low. Finally, they are taxed for capital gains like a common stock, unlike a mutual fund that must distribute net taxable gains through to you, the shareholder, despite the performance of the fund. You may invest in them based on a theme or as a hedge against an existing portfolio, or you can trade them like stocks. Investment in them is either mechanical as a hedge against another investment, purely technical as is used in a trading system, or speculative as a concentration in a specific theme.

If you insist on owning different funds, perhaps because it is easier and less expensive, the ETFs are far superior to mutual funds. Just remember that with ETFs, you still need a method to decide when to buy and when to sell as they come in and out of favor.

What Do You Do?

So, what can you do to protect and grow your financial assets? You can continue to be smooth-talked by the "professionals" and diversify into a variety of mutual funds and suffer outrageous fees, or you can do the investing yourself. To many, the do-it-yourself method is scary. Not only have they been intimidated by the pros' jargon, but they are also afraid that it requires learning a whole bunch of new things and that it may involve mathematics or other subjects they were not the best at when in school. To a slight extent, there is some basis for the fears, but not to the level that professionals would like you to believe. Most information necessary is publicly available for small fees, considerably less than any management, administrative, trust, or brokerage fees you would otherwise pay. You might have to do a little work at regular intervals, perhaps weekly or monthly, but that work shouldn't take more than an hour per session, provided the appropriate financial information is present. From this analysis, you can outperform the market averages, if history is a guide, and feel more confident that your investments are protected from substantial loss.

Why the Stock Market?

Why the stock market? Stocks have proven to be the best investment over the past 200 years. Wharton professor Jeremy Siegel calculated that in the past two centuries, the U.S. stock market had a total average return of 6.9 percent per year. This, after accounting for inflation, is often called the "real" rate of return. No other investment category has attained results even close to this outcome. The U.S. government's long-term bonds averaged 3.5 percent, and short-term bills averaged 2.9 percent over the same period. Since 1926, stocks have averaged 6.9 percent, the same as over the entire 200-year period; bond performance declined to 2.2 percent per year, and U.S. Treasury bills declined to 0.7 percent per year. The stock market results are striking. They show that stocks have worked effectively as a hedge against inflation. Inflation is with us, and it accelerated after the U.S. went off the gold standard. It is unlikely that we will return to a gold standard any time soon, and so it is probable that inflation will continue as well. It is the necessary evil of paper money.

Therefore, U.S. stocks, over the long and recent term, have been the best investment. In addition, according to Siegel, over no 30-year period have stocks ended up below their beginning prices. The presumption here is that if you can hold a stock portfolio for 30 or more years, you will always make a profit. I don't buy this thesis. First, there hasn't been many 30-year periods to arrive at a good statistical test. Second, the presumption measures only the performance of those stocks that lasted for 30 years. Finally, most people are not willing to wait 30 years to see if the theory is correct. However, it is undeniable that U.S. stocks, in general, have had a relatively high, sustained growth rate when compared to other financial assets.

By the way, when I mention holding stocks, I mean a portfolio of stocks and not necessarily putting all of your cash into an individual stock for 30 years. No one is capable of predicting anything 30 years from now. Just think of guessing who the president will be or what interest rates will be 30 years from now. Indeed, I am not confident about predicting the market even three months ahead. In addition, there are times when most investments are less than prudent; market trends rise and fall in the short term, and it is impossible to predict longer-term cycles. In some ways, it depends on how far away from the average 6.9 percent per annum the stock market is at any one moment. Siegel's calculations suggest that at any one time, the stock market can deviate substantially from the average 6.9 percent, but over time, the average of annual returns remains at the established norm. It does not suggest that the stock market, with its mean return of 6.9 percent per year for 200 years, will be up 6.9 percent each year. However, as you look at many years—some with large gains and some with large losses—you see that the overall average return was 6.9 percent. This is the basis for the argument of not worrying about market timing—trying to time the oscillations about the average to improve on the portfolio return. We explore this in more detail when we discuss specific methods for reducing capital risk.

There is also a long-term risk to the stock market. You must not put too much trust in historical figures. According to Harvard ex-professor Terry Burnham, the only stock markets over the past 200 years that have not declined to zero are the U.S. and U.K. markets. All other world markets have gone bust at some time. This suggests either that the constant rise in the U.S. market is somewhat accidental or that it is exceptionally strong and well regulated. Survival until now, however, is not a guarantee that it will survive in the future. This mislaid assumption is why many investors own stocks and won't sell them. They believe that the rise will continue forever. It will not. Therefore, we must be aware that at some time in the future, the U.S. stock market will change from its historical 6.9 percent annual growth to something considerably less and it may even decline. This is the eventual outcome of all nations and is why the "buy-and-hold" investment philosophy is ultimately flawed.

On the other hand, the rise in stock prices can continue for many years to come, and I hope it will. This is my assumption because I also introduce a simple method of protecting a portfolio from substantial capital loss during any kind of market decline. With this defensive protection method, you will not have to worry about a major market decline—short-term or permanent. In the meantime, as the stock market progresses upward, you will be able to take advantage of it.

Summary

At this point, you may be discouraged from the bad news I have given you so far. Don't give up. The good news is that there are investment methods that do work and are not difficult to use. Before we get to them, you must first come to agree with several conclusions. First, the stock market is likely the best investment arena to outperform inflation as long as you safeguard yourself from large capital losses during market declines. Second, you know you have to make investment decisions for yourself because the investment management business makes more money from you than you do on your investments with them. Third, you are left with the decision to either ride the market's ups and downs in a mutual fund or an ETF, or to select individual stock issues using a demonstrated analytical basis. I believe that the diversity provided with a mutual fund or ETF also inhibits your portfolio performance by spreading out the potential gain from individual winners: Your profit will approximate the average of all stocks in that basket, both good and bad, producing an average return. The buying and selling of individual stocks based on your own study and work has considerably more promise, and you can have fun doing it.

CHAPTER 2

BELIEFS AND BIASES

Before we continue to the ultimate goal of constructing a profitable yet relatively safe portfolio, it is important that you understand some of my beliefs and biases that have developed over the past 40 years. These beliefs come from experimenting with investment methods, watching others, (many were star portfolio managers in their day), reading academic literature on finance theory, and observing the reasons for investment mistakes that could have been avoided with common sense. To me, it is surprising how a theory without practical application or proof can disseminate through the investment world so quickly and thoroughly, only to be destroyed by the marketplace behaving normally. Whether it's stupidity, gullibility, naiveté or inattention to the peculiarities of human interaction, common sense often falls victim to popularity and hype. You must first decide whether any proposal or theory makes sense. Most theories do not make sense, and even if they do, for unexpected reasons, they often don't work in the real world anyway. Always ask for proof or evidence of success rather than apparently logical arguments.

The Markets

As mentioned earlier, I focus on the stock markets. However, most markets behave similarly. Their behavior seems to be the result of

- *Facts* that may or not be known and may or may not be accurate, such as the prospects for the economy or a specific company. This is why, for example, a company's stock historically rises in conjunction with its profits over longer periods of time, even though analysts have little idea of what those profits will be over the immediate future.
- *Anticipation* of new changes. Investors look ahead, not behind, and they compete when trying to anticipate future facts. This is why there is stiff and expensive competition among portfolio managers, analysts, and other investors to get "inside" information that is not generally known by others.
- *Emotion*, the "irrational component." Emotion comes in the form of considerable human biases that influence decision making both individually and collectively. One example is the tendency to sell winners and keep losers. People don't like to admit their errors, such as buying a stock that later declines in price. Subconsciously, they believe that by not selling that position at a loss, they are not taking a loss. However, they have no compunction against selling a profitable holding because this just demonstrates how brilliant they are. This bias is basically irrational because when practiced, a portfolio then ends up with only losers and no winners, not exactly the best way to profit. The better way to invest is the opposite: Keep winners and sell losers. Another example of irrationality is the "herd" instinct, whereby

investors tend to follow the crowd, buying into bull markets (markets rising for six months or longer) and selling into bear markets (markets declining for six months or longer) just at the wrong time when most of the price motion is ending. Strict models with specific rules and excellent performance can help avoid these emotional tugs.

The markets are the sum of all information known and anticipated, interpretation of that information, and emotional reactions to that information, right or wrong. Individuals in the market compete against some of the smartest and best financed people in the world. To beat them, you cannot use their methods. They know more and have better sources than you do; they also have methods of appraising information more quickly and accurately than you do. You cannot possibly compete in the same arena with the same information.

As an individual investor, you compete with many sources of information outside of public knowledge; you are unable to assess and predict from that information accurately; and you are often affected by emotional forces that are to some extent part of your biological makeup and out of your control. This necessitates a method that depends on facts that cannot be disputed. You must forget about attempts to predict anything and you must develop a *mechanical* process that eliminates or at least minimizes the effects of personal emotion. This process is difficult. Most of us want to predict outcomes (the ball game, the next president, the weather) and are often asked by others for our predictions. We listen to "experts" believing that they can do what we cannot, namely predict the future, but we find that they generally cannot predict the future either. We feel comfortable with the crowd and don't like standing out as oddballs or nonconformists. We have been wired to react and think over thousands of generations and have difficulty controlling these basic human emotions. In normal, everyday life, these biases can be helpful and keep us out of trouble. They help us to socialize, to accomplish group tasks, to avoid traps, to become promoted, and to live with others. In the markets, however, they can be disastrous. Portfolio managers are subject to the same biases. That's why their performances over the years have been poor and why some investment stars come and go with changes in the markets.

To avoid these difficulties, we need methods that are based on facts, are profitable with minimum capital risk, and are independent (work on their own). As you will see in later chapters, the future in markets (and in about everything else) is unpredictable. However, we can look into the past to see what methods have worked, and we can test these successful methods into the future to see if they still work. This is the principle behind successful investing. Using only methods that have profited and continue to profit is the way to succeed. They must be methods that take little human emotional intervention to avoid the risk of bias affecting decisions. They must be independent of the opinions of others. And they must be easy to implement. I will show you several methods that have profited in the past and continue to profit. These, of course, can fail in the future, but while they work, as long as there are capital safeguards, you and I can profit from them.

My Emotional Experience

I am no genius in the markets. I have made the same mistakes that everyone else has made, and I have paid for those mistakes with losses. In analyzing my own behavior, I wish to explain several behavioral problems that I have and that you should be careful not to duplicate. Most of them I have conquered, but it took a long time (and was expensive).

Impatience

One of the worst aspects of investing is impatience. When I became involved in the markets and saw prices go up and down and bemoaned the profits I could have made if I had just bought at the bottom and sold at the top, I was presented with the problem of not only figuring out how to buy at the bottom and sell at the top, but also when to do it. Eventually, I learned there wasn't a chance that I would always buy at the low and sell at the high. I realized that I had to find methods to make my odds of profit larger than my odds of loss and not try for the "home run" every time. After I determined these methods, I then had to have the patience to wait for them to signal action. If I anticipated them, I lost. If I changed my position, I lost. If I ignored them, I lost. In other words, I had to develop the patience to wait for the signal triggers to occur, and then I had to act on them, but act on them only when they occurred. The markets always go up and down, and I found that missing an opportunity would be followed sooner or later by another opportunity. It wasn't necessary to be "in" the market all the time, and indeed, I found that by trying to force profits from being in the markets at all times usually caused me to do stupid things.

Fear of Being Wrong

No human likes to be wrong, especially if that error is known to others. This can be combated in three ways: by not being wrong (which is impossible), by not telling anyone when you are wrong, or by accepting that you can be wrong occasionally and it won't kill you. Eventually, the fact of being wrong—probably because it occurs so often—no longer becomes a disgrace, especially if you are making consistent profits in spite of being wrong occasionally. Eventually, you can admit you made a mistake and not be bothered by other opinions. To get to that stage, however, takes a long time because the emotion attached to being wrong is so strong. Some people never admit to being wrong and generally they lose money in the markets (with the possible exception of one famous politician who also claims to have been commodity trader).

Looking for Perfection

Yes, there are methods of investing that seem to work. This book describes some of them. However, believing that the methods will work is another thing. I have a natural tendency to look for perfection, and when I come up with something that appears to have merit, I manipulate it to the point that it no longer works, and then I discard it. Stupid. If it works, don't fool with it until it doesn't work any longer. That's what I finally learned. Also don't expect perfection. One of the false reasons for discarding a good investment system is that it is not perfect. Some trades are unprofitable, and naturally I want all trades to be profitable even if I logically know that is impossible. If the method has a few losses, even though over time it is successful, I tended to discard it. Stupid. It has taken a long time to fight the desire for perfection and to use those methods that do work, even if they do not work perfectly.

Lack of Discipline

After I have systems that work and have only a few occasional errors, I sit and wait for a signal. When it occurs, I don't do anything. How dumb can I get? I know the method works and makes money and I know my risks of a large loss are minimal, yet I don't do anything. This is mostly due to a lack of confidence. Perhaps it won't work this time. Discipline is an overworked aspect of trading and investing and can be read about in many investment books, especially those devoted to the psychology of investing. In my case, it operates in two ways. I sit and do nothing when I should be doing something or I do something when I should be doing nothing. Sometimes this is due to impatience; I enter a position when I should be sitting or I exit a position for fear of being wrong when a position is temporarily at a loss. Sometimes it is due to fear alone, and I fail to act when I should. But, it all falls into the necessary control needed that is often called discipline. What I have found is that with a strict investment model that is profitable with minimal capital risk, I have the confidence to act when the model signals to act and my discipline is increased. I still have to fight the suspicion that "this time may be different," but the strictness and profitability of the model help considerably.

I describe these particular faults of mine because you will be subjected to the same ones and more. If you don't learn to elude them, you will have learned a perfectly good method of profiting from stock investments but will likely take large losses in your investments. Impatience, fear of being wrong, looking for perfection, and lack of discipline are normal human behavior, but they must be avoided for you to profit.

Summary

You have now been exposed to my market philosophy. That is, most conventional methods produce conventional results. Instead of following the herd of analysts and investment managers to make money in the markets, the important principles to follow are

- Markets trade on facts, anticipation of new facts, and emotion.
- Biases, such as impatience, fear of being wrong, looking for perfection, and lack of discipline, can strongly influence your investment decisions.
- Specific methods that have a history of performing well in the past are the only ones to use; never rely on rumors, friendly banter, famous advisors, or investment gurus.

There is nothing new or unique about these principles. It is surprising, however, how often they are violated or ignored.

CHAPTER 3

INVESTMENT RISK

After you decide to study the stock market because it has been the most profitable market over the long term, what aspects of investments do you need to consider? Ultimately, you have to decide how to convert these thoughts into a realistic and effective portfolio.

You not only must decide on what method to use in buying stocks, but also what to do with them when you own them. Investing is not as simple as buying and selling. Each decision must include not only the prospects for gain, but also the possibility of loss. Before we get into how to buy and sell, let's first address the problem of risk.

Individual Stock Risk

The concept of *risk* as it is used by most professionals and academics is completely wrong. Risk by their definition is *the possibility that a stock may fluctuate widely*. The possibility of capital loss is not a consideration in their calculations of performance. This concept of risk was likely created because no magic formula exists to determine whether a stock's price will rise or fall. Unbelievably, a stock trading in a flat, straight line, under this academic definition, is thought to contain little risk because it is not oscillating. By the same argument, a stock rising in price can be just as risky as a stock declining in price. This is, of course, nonsense.

Using the *standard deviation* (a statistical term measuring the amount a stock oscillates above or below its average price) is also inaccurate. You often hear or read of a *risk-adjusted return*. Although this calculation can be complicated, the most common method of recording such a thing is the Sharpe Ratio named after William Sharpe, one of the creators of the *Capital Asset Pricing Model (CAPM)*. The Sharpe Ratio determines how much better a portfolio performed than the Treasury bill rate over a specific period. It is then adjusted by this odd measure of risk. Its intention is to give an estimate of how much return was received relative to how much risk was taken. The problem is that a rising stock price (a profitable stock) has a large oscillation about its average price, and by this definition, a large risk will exist just as the result of its rise. The Sharpe Ratio and other conventional measures of risk, therefore, give equal weight to a declining stock price as to a rising stock price. The trend in the prices is not considered in these measures. Which stock would you prefer, the rising or the declining? Which stock would you consider more risky: the one declining or the one rising? Most normal people consider a rising stock price as less risky because it is increasing in value and a declining stock more risky because it is losing money. That makes sense.

As an example, let's look at the price history of hypothetical stocks A, B, and C (see Figure 3.1). Stock C rose from $20 to $80, stock B remained flat at $50, and stock A declined from $80 to $20. Which one is riskier? From a practical standpoint,

A is the most risky because it is declining. C would be the most desirable because it is rising. However, under conventional finance theory, both A and C are riskier than B because they oscillated widely above or below their average price of $50. Stock B would be the least risky because it didn't do anything, but stock C would be as risky as stock A, even though it advanced. In other words, this theory does not like volatility in either direction. It is difficult to make money when a stock's price remains the same.

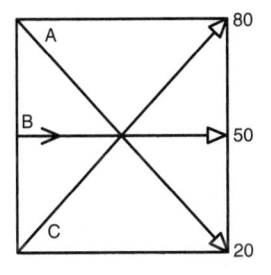

Figure 3.1
Three stock price trends

I point out this dangerous definition of risk because you need to be more concerned about losing money than about how much the stock oscillates from its mean. The two concepts are unrelated.

Randomness

Why does finance theory not consider direction of a stock price trend? Because finance theory is based on the assumption that price changes are random and don't follow trends. The market theory, called the random walk, is a popular expression of this idea. Of course, the randomness of price changes has been discredited many times by practitioners and academics, but this theory of price behavior remains embedded in other aspects of finance theory. As a practical investor desiring to profit from a rising trend, you need to be aware that risk is best equated with the possibility of capital loss and not simply with volatility. You are concerned with making money on the investment and not on how widely a stock fluctuates. Indeed, the wider a stock oscillates, the more profit it can potentially generate. Short-term traders, for example, invariably pick highly volatile stocks because wide swings equate with better profit opportunity. Nothing is more difficult to trade profitably than a "dead" stock.

Diversification

Some theorists advocate *diversification*. This theory suggests that although there may be significant risks (capital or volatility) in individual stocks due to the particular risks involved in each respective company, this risk can be significantly reduced by owning a number of different companies in different industries and dividing the risk on any one failure by the number of issues held. This theory is correct, but it is not the way to maximize profit. The problem with diversification is that it requires you to hold many different investments, some that are not particularly the best, just to reduce the chances of capital loss from "putting your eggs in one basket." By reducing the risk of capital loss, however, the diversification method also reduces the possibility of profit because it is not concentrating on the best stocks. Statistically, diversifying between industries approaches the performance of the market averages. Why not just own an S&P ETF and not worry about selection at all? I am interested in outperforming the market averages.

Using relative price strength, for example, I have found that a portfolio may hold a disproportionate share of stocks in one particular industry. This goes contrary to the thought that I should be diversified among several industries. However, if this particular industry is performing the best, and I am careful with applying my sell criteria, why shouldn't I be invested in it? The real problem, I believe, is that investors often don't have a severe sell method and get caught with losing stocks. While believing that they are protecting themselves by diversifying, they are protecting themselves from improper money management and capital risk control. Good selling criteria prevents the losses often seen in individual issues, and the likelihood of an entire industry crashing without some earlier weak price action is close to zero.

Law of Percentages

The law of percentages suggests that when an investment declines a certain percentage, it must advance by a greater percentage to get back to even. For example, if a stock declines 50 percent (say $100 to $50), it must advance 100 percent ($50 to $100) to get back to its beginning value. Having to gain 100 percent is a difficult proposition, one that can easily be avoided by not losing the 50 percent in the first place. Yet, it is surprising how many losing positions are held in professionally managed portfolios with the "hope" that they will return to their original values.

Drawdown

A more realistic measure of risk is called *drawdown*, which is calculated each time an investment declines from a new high and rises to a subsequent new high. The loss that occurred after the first new high is the drawdown. It measures how much you would have lost had you purchased the investment at its high.

As an example of drawdown, let's consider a stock that reached a high at $100, declined to $65, rallied to $80, declined to $30, and finally rose to $110. What was the drawdown during this period? It wasn't the $65 level because the drawdown is calculated from the high to the lowest point before a new high. Instead, the lowest reached from the high at $100, before the new high at $110, was not $65 but was $30. The drawdown, therefore, was 70 points ($100 at the high less $30 at the low) or 70 percent. This is a large drawdown, one that would have given your heart a slight tremor had you owned the stock during this period.

The drawdown measures how much capital loss the investment periodically suffers. It is independent of time in that the two highs can occur months or days apart. Over time and through several subsequent new highs and corrections, you can use each new drawdown to calculate an *average drawdown*. The largest of the drawdowns is called the *maximum drawdown (MDD)*. The MDD is the figure most mentioned as the potential capital risk of the investment because it represents the worst loss to have occurred.

Some analysts criticize the use of maximum drawdown as a measure of risk because it accounts only for the past price behavior in a rising market and doesn't consider future price movement. Unfortunately, this is also true of the academic risk calculations based on volatility. Standard deviations and Sharpe ratios are calculated with past data and have no predictive value either. We cannot see into the future. The advantage of using the maximum drawdown is that it accounts for deviations from a rising trend, the risk of capital loss, and the kind of price behavior we are interested in and not the volatility of the investment alone. The MDD is also used in assessing trading systems. When a trading system is developed, it produces a series of automatic buys and sells. By following a portfolio derived from these signals, the drawdown can be calculated to assess the degree of capital risk that the system generated. It is, therefore, useful in assessing the profit versus potential loss of the system.

When I discuss capital risk throughout this book, I refer to drawdown, usually maximum drawdown. A good system or investment, for example, may be volatile but have a small drawdown that would not be picked up by conventional theories of risk. That is the kind of investment worth looking for.

Market Risk

The other risk of capital loss rarely considered by professionals is the risk of capital loss from a broad market decline. The law of percentages applies equally to market risk as to any other risk category.

Market risk is the previously mentioned declines that have occurred below the central upward trend historic of 6.9 percent. These drawdowns can be substantial. Since 1885, the decline from top to bottom in the Dow Jones Industrial Average in all four-year presidential election cycles has run between 89.2 percent (1929 to 1932) to 9.68 percent (1993 to 1996). The average drawdown approximately every four years has been 30.1 percent. These are large percentages that can put your investments back a number of years before they can recuperate, even assuming an average annual, long-term gain of

6.9 percent. They occur frequently. As shown in Figure 3.2 on page 35, seven years were required for the Dow Jones Industrial peak in 2000 to be reached again. If we look at the NASDAQ, the drawdowns are even worse, and as of April 2008, it had not yet returned to its 2000 peak. After the peak in 1929, 25 years passed before stock prices exceeded that peak, and the drawdown was almost 90 percent. Can this occur again? Of course it can. To think otherwise is unrealistic.

In market declines, all stocks are hit, including big stocks, little stocks, industry-specific stocks, and foreign stocks, suggesting that diversification between countries or stocks is not an adequate hedge against market risk. A good example is the decline in the month of January 2008, when all over the world, stock markets declined at roughly the same pace. The best and safest method to mitigate this risk is to have some kind of bailout point below which all stocks are sold. Even if the market turns back upward immediately, your portfolio will have lost only a small portion of its value but prevented the unknown further decline from harming your capital.

Most portfolio managers prefer to keep a constant ratio of stocks to cash or bonds, and most mutual funds tend to keep close to 100 percent invested at all times. This means that the portfolio will oscillate in the direction of the market and lose value during a market decline. This investment tendency prevents them from selling to protect against a further decline. Although it is difficult to predict a decline, a portfolio can react to a decline and still avoid a major loss. This is not done in most portfolios because the sales department wants the portfolio fully invested to please potential customers. (No one wants to buy a fund invested in cash.) You might withdraw your capital if you see that the fund is not close to 100 percent invested.

Investment Risk

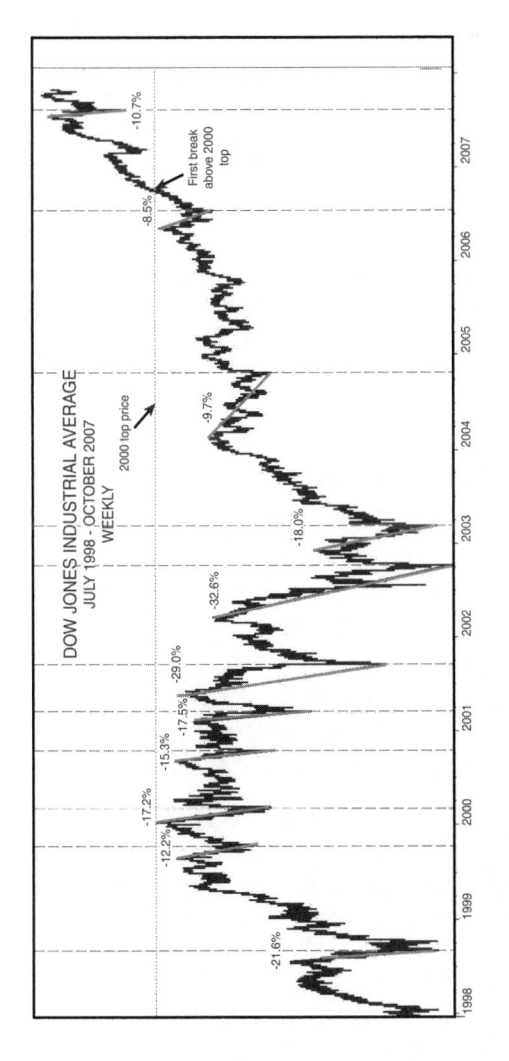

Figure 3.2
Market declines for the past 10 years

Charging for investment management is one thing, but charging for holding cash is usually not acceptable to the mutual fund investor.

Some managers use derivatives such as S&P 500 futures or options to hedge their portfolios; they may also diversify by using ETFs in place of single stock positions. But these hedges just slow any advance. The easiest and cleanest method to avoid loss is to raise cash. Indeed, the ideal portfolio should work from the proposition that cash is the primary investment (because it is riskless, except for inflation and currency deterioration) and that investments are purchased only as they become potentially profitable.

DEFINITIONS

Leverage is a term used to describe the ratio of the value of an invested position to your own capital in the position. A leverage of 2 to 1, for example, describes an investment that is worth $2 and in which you have invested $1. The other $1 is borrowed. A leverage of 20 to 1 describes an investment worth $20 to your position of $1 dollar and is especially risky because if the investment declines only $1 dollar, you lose your entire position. High leverage makes an investment more vulnerable to failure.

Liquidity refers to the ease with which an investment can be bought and sold. If a stock is liquid, it trades many shares and is easily bought and sold. Liquidity can depend on many factors and is never a constant. A *liquidity squeeze* occurs when an investment has little or no liquidity. If you are forced to buy or sell it to cover a position or repay a loan, for example, you would not receive a good price for your order.

The principle argument uses against selling stocks in preparation for a decline is lack of liquidity or the lack of sufficient volume buyers to absorb large positions. Even then, under normal circumstances, not a panic, a large portfolio can be liquidated easily. I had a customer and friend more than 20 years ago who managed one of the largest mutual funds at the time. He decided to test market liquidity and successfully sold and bought back his entire portfolio within a week with negligible effect on its performance. Liquidity is not a problem for the average investor. Millions of shares trade every day, and the relatively small order size of the average investor is unlikely to affect market prices.

Summary

So far, I have explained why

- Stocks are the best investments.
- You can do better investing in stocks than in mutual funds.
- You can perform your own analyses.
- Risk is improperly defined, and you are wise to be wary of capital loss in stocks.
- You do not need to worry about oscillations or price volatility.
- You should be aware of your own biases and learn to recognize and control them.

CHAPTER 4

CONVENTIONAL ANALYSIS

If you make your own investment decisions, you need to understand the methods available, especially those that have worked in the past, even if they go against your intuition.

Fundamental Versus Technical Methods

The two basic methods of analyzing stocks are *fundamental* and *technical*. Fundamental analysis is based on attempting to predict a security's price outcome from capital and sales trends, and technical analysis is based on reacting to a security's price behavior. Their philosophies differ in many other ways. For example, the technical approach is not interested in the security's underlying value, whereas the fundamental analyst is obsessed with it. The fundamentalists believe that if they can determine what a stock's "true" value is, and that value is more than how the market is pricing the security, there is an opportunity for profit when the market finally recognizes that true value. This method is diametrically opposite from technical analysis, which believes the market already knows the value of the stock because it has already adjusted for current analyst thinking and belief, hope, greed, fear, inside information, and speculation. This is a more humble approach and is why most technicians do not develop unreasonable attachments to individual securities and their respective companies. It permits them to become more objective about prospects for a security (where you make your money) rather than for the underlying company.

Fundamental Method

The fundamental analyst studies the corporation's financial strength and performance. This analyst considers many factors such as earnings, balance sheet values, dividends, growth rate, markets, products, management, and competition. The result of this study is the determination of the growth potential of the company and a predicted market value. From this conclusion, the fundamental analyst calculates the ideal price of the stock by using ratios based on stock or market history. If the market price of the stock is far below its predicted value price, the stock is presumed to be a buy. If the market price is far above the predicted value, the stock must be a sale.

This method assumes that the analysis is correct and that the information gathered for that analysis is accurate. Unfortunately, these assumptions can be wrong. For example, many analysts were duped by the Enron management and kept recommending purchase of the stock long after insiders were selling. Someone knew the story was phony because the stock price was declining. To the fundamental analyst who was calculating with incorrect information, each tick downward pointed to the stock as a better buy, until, of course, it was revealed that the information was inaccurate. This method also assumes that the analyst knows more than the market about how to price the stock. It assumes an egotistical attitude in the face of an analysis of complex and unquantifiable data. How, for example, do you determine management quantitatively, or competition, or growth prospects, or markets? It can't be done and is one reason why the history of analyst earnings estimates is so dismal.

Technical Analysis

The other approach to analysis is the technical method. This method originally began with the study of market price action and then expanded to individual stock price action. At first, market observers like Charles Dow, founder of The Dow Jones Company and the *Wall Street Journal*, considered price averages to be a reflection of future economic prospects. Later, in the days of the robber barons, when the average Joe had no idea what the barons were doing when manipulating stock prices as they competed with each other for ownership, it became obvious that certain patterns in stock price behavior developed when the barons were accumulating or distributing stock. These patterns were believed to have some predictive value and could be used to make decisions when there was little or no accurate fundamental information. Prices were always accurate, but other information was not. Technical analysis, therefore, grew as a method for the little guy, who was not privileged with inside information, to compete in the big guy's world.

The theory behind technical analysis today is quite basic. It assumes that stock prices, similar to other goods and services, follow the economic principle of supply and demand for stock. Supply and demand are determined by many factors, most of which are indeterminable but include information, anticipation, and emotion. The old-timers found that prices often formed patterns, recognizable in charts (technical analysts are often incorrectly called *chartists*) and tended to travel in trends. They also found that prices don't trend all the time. Indeed, they trend only for relatively short periods, usually between three months to a year. This is useful information, however, because it suggests that if the investor can determine the beginning of a new trend, he can often profit from the trend as long as it lasts. Most technical analysis of prices for investment is now focused on determining how to recognize when a new price trend has begun. Charts are still used, but computers have replaced them in most studies of price behavior.

EMH and Other Useless Theories

No discussion of the markets would be complete without discussing, even briefly, the *efficient markets hypothesis (EMH)*. This is a hypothesis developed in academia to describe the marketplace as something unpredictable and impossible to profit from. To some extent academics are correct in theorizing that making money in the markets is difficult. It is, but not because of finance theory. It is difficult because it requires strict mental discipline to follow only rules that have worked in the past and to avoid all the emotional attachments and biases so common to human beings.

These academic theories are convenient for their adherents, of course, because they cannot be proven wrong (or right). However, they also have little connection with reality. When "experts" use these theories in the real world, often they end up with nothing.

The principles of inductive logic state that one example of a failure refutes the entire theory. University of Massachusetts Professor Nassim Taleb calls these failures "Black Swans" from the sighting of a black swan during the discovery of Australia.

Conventional Analysis

"One single observation can invalidate a general statement (all swans are white) derived from millennia of confirmatory sightings of millions of white swans." Similarly, the failure of finance theory comes from an unexpected event that is not accounted for in the theory. These failures, along with too much borrowed money, have caused several notable failures and collapses for adherents to the efficient markets hypothesis.

One example in recent times of a black swan destroying believers in the efficient markets hypothesis is the Long Term Capital Management (LTCM) collapse. This fund, formed in 1994, included two famous Nobel-prize winning finance professors as principals, as well as others. By 1998, when it collapsed, it had borrowed almost $125 billion against around $4.7 billion in assets to execute complex mathematical models based on finance theory. In addition, it had off-balance sheet liabilities (not reported on their statements) of more than $1.25 trillion. It was at first successful, making around 40 percent per year, but as its assets grew, it needed to find more obscure methods of investing utilizing the finance theory.

Efficient market strategies often employ the belief that when securities become out of balance with others, arbitration can bring the prices back to their normal relationship. Deviations from historic patterns would return to normal after temporary dislocations. But this is not always so or immediate.

Royal Dutch/Shell is an easy and much studied example. Royal Dutch/Shell trades in two exchanges, the U.S. and the Netherlands. The shares traded in both markets are identical, and the only difference is that they trade on different stock exchanges in different currencies. If the U.S. stock price becomes higher than the Netherlands price, adjusted for the currency difference, a riskless opportunity arises. Because the shares are identical, they should revert to exactly the same market price. Theoretically, stock should be sold in the United States and purchased in the Netherlands for the gain existing in the market difference, bringing the two prices into equilibrium. This buy/sell transaction is called "putting on a spread" and eventually should become profitable. As it turns out, this doesn't work for a number of reasons, and is even more disastrous if the spread widens as the price difference increases. This flaw in arbitration is another demonstration that the EMH has problems.

In these types of trades, because the spreads have small profit margins, LTCM borrowed large sums of money on the idea that by making small profits on large positions, it could continue making large overall gains. In 1998, an arbitrage existed between U.S. and foreign bonds. The fund made a large bet by selling short U.S. government bonds and buying long many foreign bonds, envisaging that it would profit from the prices converging. (U.S. bonds would decline and foreign bonds advance.) They had studied the price of U.S. bonds versus foreign bonds and found that their market prices had a current spread wider than in the past and under finance theory, they would reap the benefit of the price returning into balance. There would be little risk because this return to equilibrium had always occurred. Then, Russia defaulted on its bonds. These were not in the LTCM portfolio and were assumed to be unrelated to its foreign bond holding. However, investors sold all foreign bonds in a "flight to quality," not just Russian bonds, in favor of buying U.S. bonds, just the opposite of the fund's strategy. This was the unexpected black swan. Investors didn't arbitrate like they had in the past. They panicked instead. By August, 1998, LTCM had lost approximately $2 billion of its own capital, and by September, it had only $600 million in net assets and billions in liabilities. Eventually, the Federal Reserve assisted banks to save the financial system from collapse by buying out LTCM's positions to be liquidated over time. Ironically, after LTCM was liquidated, and the markets settled down, its original positions would have been profitable. Its problem was twofold: Using finance theory, it miscalculated its estimates of correlations between U.S. and foreign bond prices, and using too much leverage (borrowed money), it was unable to withstand an unexpected liquidity squeeze. The black swan destroyed its assumption of minimum financial risk.

The EMH centers on several unrealistic assumptions. First, it assumes that prices oscillate in a random fashion; that is, they are unpredictable and have no trend. Professors Andrew Lo and Craig MacKinley, from MIT and Wharton, respectively, have shown mathematically that stock prices are not random.

Second, it assumes that prices change instantly and only on new and developing information. A considerable problem for the EMH arose, for example, when the large and sudden decline in 1987 had no news accompanying it.

Third, it assumes that information is disseminated instantly and is correctly analyzed and immediately acted upon. Of course, this is absurd. You are often the last person to learn of any change in information. You also cannot possibly assimilate all the news in the universe every second and assess its significance instantaneously and then act upon it. It is a well-founded behavioral principle that the human mind cannot assimilate and analyze more than a few variables at one time and must resort to instinct or experience when overloaded with information. These instinctual reactions are often incorrect, and decisions, especially in the uncertainty of the marketplace, are often incorrect. In addition, you have to sleep sometime.

Finally, it assumes that the analysis will be based on reason, what the "rational" person would do. This is equally absurd when we see how irrational investors can become—for example, during bubbles and panics. Who would have thought that a decline in Russian bonds would cause a decline in other foreign bonds? Recently, academia has found through experiment many quirks in human psychological behavior that could be defined as irrational, at least in the marketplace. Earlier, I mentioned the tendency to sell profitable stocks and hold onto unprofitable stocks. This is irrational. Being affected by stock manias, up or down, is irrational. Investing on what you hear during cocktail chatter or in the golf club locker room is irrational. Would you buy chocolate coins if someone at a dinner party recommended them as an investment? Some irrational people would.

Unbelievably some professionals still stick to these academic hypotheses and theories, but less and less. The more advanced portfolio managers have long believed these hypotheses are nonsense and do not utilize them at all. Someday MBA programs will also realize they are teaching fallacious hypotheses to their students and will help rather than hinder them to understand the practical aspects of the markets.

Summary

Conventional analysis has its faults. Fundamental analysis is difficult to achieve accurately and implies knowledge greater than the market place. Technical analysis avoids the problem of prediction (although many technical analysts fall into the trap of predicting) and instead reacts, to the market. Finally, the Efficient Markets Hypothesis is an idea that appeals to academics but is completely impractical in the real world of markets. You should be wary of any of these methods, especially if proof of profitability is lacking.

CHAPTER 5

PREDICTION VERSUS REACTION

Never, never, never try to predict the markets. Most professionals with considerably more timely and accurate information than you cannot predict the markets. You don't stand a chance. This is difficult to accept. Most people are wired to expect a certain future path and then to follow it. Nothing could be more harmful in the markets. Not only will your prediction likely be wrong, but also your mind will be stuck on that prediction and have difficulty accepting that it may be wrong. Behavioral finance students have long known that people get fixated on numbers and tend to focus on those numbers in their expectations, even when the numbers are totally unrealistic. Don't make predictions.

Economists

Economists use economic, demographic, political, and other large-scale data, and over the years they have developed models of the economy based on the interaction of this data. I remember taking an advanced economics course at Harvard called Econometric Modeling and Forecasting. It was taught by a leading academic economist of the time. The course made the subject of forecasting the economy appear to be easy using multiple variables in a regression formula. Unfortunately, even 40 years later, economists still have a dismal record of anticipating the economy. The *Wall Street Journal* takes annual polls of economists' predictions and compares them to what actually happened a year later. As an example, out of 56 economic forecasters in the first and second quarter of 2001, only two correctly predicted GNP growth for the following quarter. Their average error was 2.6 percent for an economy only growing at 4.0 percent. An academic study by University of Alabama professors Robert Brooks and Brian Gray also found that the analyses shows the consensus forecast of U.S. Treasury bond yield change is poor and a naïve forecast is more accurate.

A more recent 2006 study of the inaccuracies in economist forecasts is reported by Michael Mandel, chief economic editor for *BusinessWeek* magazine. Out of 14 years of *BusinessWeek* surveys, "There were six years when actual growth fell outside the range between high and low." In other words, the predictions by economists for the following year's GDP were so incorrect that the final GDP was different from all economists' forecasts in those six years. That means that during the entire 14 years, 40 percent of all economists were wrong in their estimates. How useful, therefore, are their estimates today? Not much.

Although unquestionably some connection exists between economic data and the stock and bond markets, it seems no one has come up with a reliable answer as to how it works. In addition to changes in the relationships between data sources and their reliability, a lag often exists between one set and another. For example, we don't know what the economy is doing right now and will only know some months down the road when the results are available. It is often said that the stock market leads the economy, and it often does. The economy then is a lagging indicator—it lags behind the stock market, which has already anticipated the economy's strength or weakness. The stock market is based on expectations, not on history. Investors buy a stock because they expect it to rise, not because it has already risen. (This is not quite true because we now know that there is a positive feedback from a rising stock price that incites investors to buy more.) Why should we spend so much time in analyzing a lagging indicator (the economy), which even the highly paid experts cannot predict, to forecast a leading indicator (the stock market), something that has already adjusted to actual, ongoing, economic changes? Discussion of the economy with regard to investments, therefore, has never made sense to me. Odds favor the investor losing money from listening to the economists.

Gurus and "Experts"

Stock market experts come in many varieties. Some are connected with brokerage firms as *market strategists*, many write newsletters on the market, and many others write articles in magazines on a regular basis. Snapshot, a thorough study of publicly available predictions by 47 different "experts" (www.CXOadvisory.com), found that only 48 percent of them were accurate in their forecasts. This isn't even as good as flipping a coin. They admitted that some were better than others were, but also that some famous names appeared at the list's bottom.

For many years, Investor Intelligence Inc. (www.investorsintelligence.com) has reviewed on a weekly basis the direction of the stock market anticipated by newsletter writers and investment advisors. They found that when a preponderance of these professional analysts agrees on the direction of the market, the market inevitably reverses direction from what is expected. Their service is useful in that it signals when advisors are too much of the same opinion and thus when the stock market will likely prove them wrong. This is a sorry commentary on these professionals because it suggests they are mostly wrong at major market turning points.

Commentator and chief market strategist Barry Ritholtz states that the SEC should require all analyst and pundit forecasts with the following: *"The undersigned states that he has no idea what's going to happen in the future, and hereby declares that this prediction is merely a wildly unsupported speculation."*

Mutual Funds

From numerous studies we know that portfolio managers have a poor track record when compared with the stock market at large. In Chapter 1, "Investing Today," I explained how the average mutual fund falls approximately 2 percent below the average performance of the stock market. I also have seen that mutual funds are more interested in their fees than in your performance and take a substantial portion of your investment for performing poorly. Finally, I know that mutual funds are reticent to sell stocks in a decline for fear of losing investors in their funds. In sum, they do little for you, increase the risk of capital loss, and charge you handsomely for it.

Security Analysts

The methods of determining fundamental predicted value in securities depend on data that is generally not timely or accurate.

For example, one popular model estimates the present value of discounted future cash flow. This model estimates what cash flow the underlying company will generate over a period of years and back-adjusts that cash flow to the present, based on an estimate of the prevailing interest rate over those years. Now please! How can anyone predict future cash flows for a period of years and then discount them by a predicted interest rate when both predictions are likely wrong? Interest rates cannot be predicted by anyone, and earnings or cash flow estimates are going to be equally as unreliable. How then do you expect to combine two unpredictable factors into one reliable estimate? It's nonsense.

In a study of 78,695 earnings forecasts over the 20-year period between 1973 and 1993, David Dreman, chairman of the Dreman Value Fund and founder of the *Journal of Psychology and Financial Markets*, demonstrated that only one in 170 analyst forecasts were within 5 percent of any four consecutive quarter's actual earnings. That's a miserable record and demonstrates the pointlessness of attempting to predict earnings out even one year. Think of the money wasted by major brokerage houses and research departments of management companies on such endeavors. No wonder their performance is mediocre.

Several studies have confirmed that earnings estimates have another problem unrelated to the actual data used in their calculation. Professors Elgers, Lo, and Pfeiffer in *Accounting Review* say, "Analysts' forecasts are not necessarily better representations of the security market's earnings expectations than are time-series or security price-based forecasts." This means that analyst forecasts would be just as accurate from projecting past earnings in a straight line without any analysis.

Several studies also have shown that security analysts have a strong bias toward inflating estimates to curry favor with management. They want to be seen as "friendly" to management both for inside or first-call information and perhaps for underwriting business for their firm. When they come out with an unfavorable earnings estimate, they are often blackballed by the company management, and in some cases, have even been sued.

Finally, there is always the possibility of fraudulent information. My favorite fraud story, told to me by the now deceased son of one of the participants, is not the Enron fraud but one that was never discovered (that I know of). It is a story of creating false information to bolster a specific bond price. Over a large river in an undisclosed location on the East Coast, a toll bridge was built to ease traffic in the area. This bridge was financed by a tax-free municipal bond underwriting predominately held by an investment banker. Many years later, the state decided to build a wider, toll-free bridge down river from the old bridge. Traffic was diverted to the new bridge, and the revenues of the old bridge declined to the point where the bonds might have to default. Mysteriously, during a particularly windy storm one night, several barges broke loose upriver and crashed into the new bridge, causing considerable damage that took almost a year to repair. Naturally, the traffic reverted to the old bridge; toll revenues increased again; the bonds recovered; and the investment banker sold them. Lesson: Always be careful when scrutinizing income flow because it may be manipulated to influence the price of the security.

As opposed to the possible inaccuracies in fundamental information, technical data is current and consists of usually reliable price data. The analyst, however, must decipher exactly what the price gyrations imply for the future. This can be done, but only with extreme skill and experience. Many technical theories are also nonsense and are yet to be demonstrated to contain any proof of profitability.

Reaction Technique

Stock price prediction is a futile effort. The errors are too large and the history of failures too long. Many economists, gurus, and pundits make good livings out of predicting, but their records are rarely scrutinized closely. If they are, the results are surprisingly poor. Does this imply that buying and selling stocks is a futile endeavor? No! The more successful alternative to prediction in the investment markets is "reaction."

Reaction refers to waiting for the market to indicate what it is going to do. Reacting requires current and reliable data (technical or fundamental), and doesn't try to estimate the precise consequences of that data. Stock prices are the best data because they are generally reported accurately, and reported company data is semireliable. Reaction occurs only when the data shows a pattern, not necessarily technical, that has been successful in the past.

Reaction takes place in three steps: the setup, the trigger, and the action (STRACT). It takes patience to wait for the setup and speed to act when the trigger "snaps." Let's look at a STRACT example. Suppose you study stock prices and find that when stocks advance to a new 52-week high, their chances of continuing higher by 10 percent are 70 percent (this is a made-up example, not to be used in the real market). You decide these are good odds. To use the reaction technique, suppose you follow 100 stocks, watching their prices. Let's say 20 of the stocks have been rising and are close to their old highs. This is the setup. You should watch those 20 stocks and not waste time with the others unless one or two also rise close to their previous highs. You now wait patiently for the trigger. For this example, that comes when a stock trades at a new high. The trigger tells you to act and your action is buying the stock. Presumably, you have already decided how much to buy while you were waiting for the trigger, and after the trigger occurs, you act quickly to take advantage of your study of new highs.

STRACT is not limited to price data alone, though price data is usually more accurate than other data. Fundamental data can also be used to create setups and triggers. The data, however, must be current and reliable, and it must be data reported by the respective company, not an estimate of future data. Because future projections are so unreliable, they are useless in a reaction technique. In addition, the relationship involved in the specific reaction must be tested for reliability and potential loss. Excellent data is useless if you don't have a reliable, profitable, fully tested method of using it.

When action occurs and you own a stock, the STRACT method switches to those criteria that tell you the best time to sell the stock. Again, as in the buy reaction, you wait until the signs appear that the stock rise is ending. In the previous example, you might have discovered that when your selected stocks, after being purchased, fail to reach new highs within 10 days, they generally underperform the market. The STRACT setup begins on the purchase of the stock from the preceding buying rule and continues when the stocks fail to reach new highs. The trigger is on the tenth day of failure. The action is to sell those stocks being triggered by the rule. This is your sell reaction. You don't predict when that end may be—it could be next week or next year. You don't really care because you are in a stock that presumably is rising and will be sold when it begins to fail. In this manner, the entire futile effort involved in predicting is eliminated. You hold the stock and let the market decide when you should sell. The whole process of buying and selling is based on proven methods and easily available data. You don't need predictions of earnings, price, time to hold, and so forth.

The question now is, "What are some methods that have worked?" What information or calculations do you need to create a STRACT setup, and what are the triggers for both buying and selling? I will show you several tests of methods I have used over the past 25 years. One model has been publicly published each week since 1982 and another, better model, has been published since 1998. These models performed well. You will be given the additional specific methods derived from these tests that could potentially improve earlier models. From there, I will show you several ways to create a portfolio that you can manage by yourself that will also prevent major losses in the case of large market declines.

Summary

Most investors don't seem to realize that the information and especially the opinions they receive are inaccurate or at the very best random. The opinions of economists, gurus, security analysts, and mutual fund managers are as accurate as flipping a coin. Of course, many of these people make large salaries and sound impressive when speaking on TV, but close scrutiny of their results show that they are just average folks. With estimates suspect, and information potentially inaccurate, the only way I know to make money is to forget about predicting and instead to react to the market itself with the STRACT technique. This means that tested methods are utilized when certain setups occur and trigger some kind of action. At other times, when a setup is unavailable, the investor just waits until circumstances become favorable again. It is an easy technique, has buy and sell triggers, and capital risk safeguards, and its analysis can be finished in short periods of time.

Chapter 6

Meeting the Relatives

Your first investment problem is deciding what to buy and how to do so without having to predict anything. You should first find available fundamental and technical data from the immediate past. When that data is combined with the following methods, you are ready to develop a STRACT setup and trigger to buy.

The three principal methods for selecting stocks are Value, Growth, and Price Strength. Value and Growth require accurate company fundamental data for each stock that is in your universe of potential stocks. Price Strength measures how a stock price behaves against its immediate past and requires a history of prices for each stock. If a stock is high versus its immediate past, it is said to have strength.

The method I use looks at "relative" data—that is, data compared to other data—rather than just the data itself. For example, when I study value, I look not only at the value of the company, but also at its value relative to the value of all other companies. I can pick a company with good value, but to maximize my investment return, I also need to look at only those companies with the best value. As for stock strength, I look at a stock's strength relative to the strength of all other stocks.

This is the basis for investing with relatives.

Value

Think of adding the value of all you own—your house, car, personal items, stocks and bonds, and so forth—and what you could sell it for, and then subtract from that figure all your debt (such as mortgage, credit cards, and so on). The result is your net value, or *net worth*.

For a company, you can do the same thing. You need to know the total liabilities and total assets for each company, as well as the number of shares it has outstanding. This information is available at many free websites. Value is determined by subtracting the liabilities of a company from its assets and dividing that number by the number of shares outstanding to give you net asset value per share of stock for that company. When you compare this share value to the stock's market price, you will see that it is either above or below that price. Usually there is a reason for any difference, but you likely won't know what it is. Anyone can do this calculation, so any difference must be explained by some other factors that are not immediately apparent. In theory, if a company owns considerable assets, such as a mining or oil company, this method will have more substance than using it for a company with few assets, such as a software or a financial services company.

Generally, *net asset value*, also called *book value* because the company's total assets and liabilities are taken directly from the company's books, is not a good or specific enough method to be useful for investing. The assets often are not valued at the market. Land, for example, is always valued at its original cost, not what it might be worth if sold today, which might be considerably higher. Machinery and buildings are valued at their depreciated cost, not at what they might bring in the marketplace. Thus, the valuation of assets, if read directly from a company's balance sheet, is incorrect and not a realistic measure of the company's value. It is also difficult to use in comparing one company with another. How would you look at two companies with different net asset values and determine from that information alone whether one or the other company is better than the other?

Rather than a value based strictly on assets and liabilities, a better test is the *ratio method*. This method uses a ratio of the current price to some aspect of the earnings of the company. The most common is the *price-to-earnings ratio*. Rather than using assets and liabilities, this method uses the earnings power of the company. It can be universally applied.

DEFINITIONS

In comparative analysis of one stock to others, most comparisons use data *per share*. Earnings for a company are earnings per share—the total earnings divided by the number of shares outstanding. The term *price earnings ratio* refers to the company's stock price divided by its earnings per share.

Generally, the lower the ratio, the more value you get for your money and the better chances you get for the value to increase if earnings expand. The principal problem with this method is determining which value to relate to price. Rather than earnings in the denominator of the ratio to price, you can use other aspects of earnings. For example, I use the price-to-sales ratio (that is, the stock price divided by the total company sales per share) rather than the price-to-earnings ratio in estimating value. Although sales figures can also be manipulated, they are generally more accurate than earnings because earnings figures include many more variables that can be adjusted. Sales figures can be pushed forward or backward, adjusted for currency translation, and so on, but still they are more accurate than other measures. Some other ratios I have disregarded are price-to-cost-of-goods sold, price-to-cash flow, and price-to-expenses.

If you want to compare one company to another using ratios, do you take current figures as reported by the company or do you take future estimates by security analysts? Both sets of earnings are publicly available. However, evidence shows that estimates are often inaccurate, certainly more so than reported figures. I use only reported sales figures and leave the estimates to others.

The other problem is that value changes for specific companies as the stock market rises and falls. The value ratio today may be considerably different from the value last year. Which one is the most realistic? The only way to combat this problem is to measure the ratio of each company relative to each other company. That way the influence of the entire market is reduced, and you can look for those companies with value ratios lower than other companies.

The method I use in determining relative value is to take the price-to-sales ratio for every company that has stock in my universe of 8,000 U.S. stocks and compare it to the same ratio of all other companies. That way, I have a reliable, consistent method for determining those companies that are trading at low valuations relative to the rest of the market.

Growth

As opposed to determining whether a company stock is undervalued against either its net assets or its existing earnings, the growth method looks for changes in earnings. It assumes that a growing company will have higher and higher valuations in the future as earnings accumulate. The problem then is to find those companies that have that high growth in earnings. If you can find companies that have high earnings growth and that have low relative valuation in the market, presumably you will have an investment opportunity. As the growth develops, the stock price should rise accordingly. In addition, those stocks with low relative value that have high earnings growth are more likely to have a sharper rise, especially when positive "earnings surprises" are announced. The low valuation indicates that strong growth is not expected and thus becomes a favorable surprise if it occurs.

A number of methods determine the growth of a company through its earnings, and most methods become too complicated. When used with inaccurate earnings estimates, they become useless. The only method I have found to measure the growth of a company, and I have doubts about it, too, is to take a company's reported earnings over the immediate past and assume the earnings trend will continue and at a similar rate. This is risky, of course, because reported earnings are always subject to error. In addition, to assume they will continue at the same rate is a form of prediction that I prefer to avoid. I am not alone. Being a potentially profitable exercise, many academics and professionals have studied the price performance results from selecting stocks based on their relative growth. In those studies using predicted data, the investment results have been poor because of the difficulty in predicting accurately.

Let me tell an anecdote about earnings and price behavior. I was once an expert witness in federal court on a case that involved a class action suit against a NYSE-listed company. The complainants argued that the stock of this company declined before an announcement of poor earnings and that the loss from holding the stock during that period was the difference between the price of the shares on the day of the announcement and the day it began to decline. They were suggesting that insiders had leaked the poor earnings early and that those not in the know suffered unfairly. My testimony was to show that stock prices can rise or fall regardless of earnings and that the decline in the stock could have been due to many factors. I demonstrated this by creating a table of past several quarters' earnings in five major companies and the subsequent stock price action. I covered with my hand the stock price action and asked the court to tell me from the future earnings displayed on the table, pretending they had perfect foreknowledge of the earnings ahead of the price action, what would they have done with the stock. I lifted my hand and showed that companies with increasing earnings declined in price and those with declining earnings rose in price, demonstrating that earnings don't necessarily determine future prices over the immediate future. The complainants were not happy with my presentation and eventually lost the case, perhaps somewhat due to my display about earnings and prices. My point here is that many analysts and investors assume that the primary determinant of future stock prices is the company's earnings. This is not so. Perfect knowledge ahead will not necessarily be profitable.

In the more successful academic studies of growth and price action, the prediction component was eliminated by taking only data that was known at the time and discarding all predicted data (knowledge ahead). In addition to reported earnings growth, these studies include relative revenue volatility (the amount by which total company sales oscillate), earnings changes, and cost of goods sold as a percentage of sales. Most of these studies have shown solid statistically significant results.

Price Strength

Relative price strength, or simply *relative strength,* is the relationship between a stock price today versus its past. A strong stock, for example, is higher than it has been in the immediate past. Relative price strength is the comparison of one stock's price strength to that of other stocks. The concept of relative strength has been controversial.

First, it is counterintuitive and difficult to accept. It is based on the observation that strong stocks tend to remain strong, and weak stocks tend to remain weak. Most investors are nervous about buying a strong stock because it has already risen at a fast rate and much of the profit apparently has already occurred. It is difficult for them to buy such a stock, even though the odds are in favor of the strong stock over the declining stock. Most people think of buying stocks similarly to how they shop for items in a store. They desire a bargain, a discount, or the feeling that they are taking advantage of a situation. It is psychologically difficult to buy something at its highest price, especially if the price has run up recently. It is counterintuitive to buy stocks that are rapidly advancing. Instead, the most common desire is to buy stocks that are declining, hoping to get a bargain when the stock hits bottom. Unfortunately, there is usually a reason for the stock's decline, and studies of price behavior demonstrate that the odds are significantly in favor of that decline continuing. To act on the relative strength of stocks is to act against your innate nature. It is difficult to get over this bias toward wanting a bargain price.

Second, relative price strength usually is useful mostly for periods shorter than a year. That is sooner than you probably desire for your investments. You are more likely to want to hold your investments for more than a year to take advantage of the tax laws on capital gains. Many investors are paranoid about paying taxes and allow their investments to suffer to avoid them. I am quite confident that this obsession with holding for a year is unrealistic. If only 1 out 170 analysts can predict earnings out a year ahead, economists cannot predict the economy a year ahead, and most investment gurus are right only 50 percent of the time, selecting a stock to perform and holding it for a year or more, based on their information and analyses, is a questionable approach.

The holding period for a stock bought on relative strength often is indeterminable at the beginning. It could remain strong for only a week or for over a year. It is only sold when the STRACT sell rule triggers regardless of the period and the direction of the general market. This means that the strong stock must be recognized early and jumped on immediately to even reap a short-term gain. The reason for this tendency to remain strong, even for a relatively short period, is recognized by most technical analysts. They have observed that stocks tend to travel in trends—up, down, or sideways—over periods up to a year. Some stocks travel in trends for considerably longer than a year, but it is almost impossible to determine how lengthy the trend will be at its beginning. If stocks have this tendency to trend, those stocks with the steepest upward trend should be the best performers, right? That's the reason that relative strength tends to profit. It selects those stocks that are trending at the steepest upward rate, the ones that will continue and have the most profit potential. Of course, the upward trend will not last forever, and fortunately when it approaches its end, measures of relative price strength warn that the upward price momentum is waning, signaling that the stock should likely be sold. Thus, relative price strength can be used as both a buy and sell criteria for investing.

The historic problem with most relative strength calculations is the period over which the price strength is measured. This is because the trend will end at some time. It pays to find that trend early but, on the other hand, not so early that the investor is buying just an oscillation in another longer trend, perhaps even a downward trend. This determination is tricky, and many experiments have been performed as to what time period should be used. The best result of those tests is that relative strength should be calculated over the preceding six months. This has been confirmed in the industry and in academia. Any shorter period produces poor results, because it falsely picks up short-term oscillations, and any longer period raises the risk that most of the action has occurred, and thus the trend is ending.

PERCENTILES

A list divided into *percentiles* is first sorted by a number or name (for example, by relative price strength) and divided into 100 sections of equal number in each section. I label percentiles between 99 and zero. The top section, the highest percentile, is 99, the next is 98 and so on until the last section, which is zero. and the lowest section is zero. Using percentiles is a way of simplifying large amounts of data into fewer cross-sections. There may be thousands of observations in each percentile. In this study, I looked at almost 300,000 observations. With roughly 300,000 observations per percentile, studying percentiles was much easier than studying each observation.

Academia has studied relative price strength and is not sure how to deal with it because its success suggests that the markets are not efficient and that, therefore, academic theories of the efficient markets hypothesis and random walk theory are in doubt. The earliest published study was by Robert A. Levy for his doctoral thesis at American University. Later, in 1968, he published an article in the *Journal of Finance* describing his findings. His method was to calculate the relative strength for each stock by dividing the 131-day moving average of the price closes for each stock in his universe by the last closing price. He then ranked the entire list by percentiles to ease the calculations, similar to what I have done with the other relatives. He found there was a direct correlation between the relative price strength percentile ranking and the performance of the stock six months afterward. Unfortunately, his method was severely criticized at the time. Academia had just become enamored over the efficient markets hypothesis and wouldn't accept any evidence to the contrary. Harvard professor, Michael Jensen, and University of Rochester professor, George Bennington, in a subsequent article in the *Journal of Finance* refuted Levy's article by arguing that Levy had omitted commission costs, which, if included, would have invalidated his findings. I came across Bob Levy's theory in early 1970 when I worked at Arthur Lipper Corp in New York as a technical analyst. Bob had befriended Arthur Lipper who gave him a small retainer to keep him producing ideas for the firm. Bob and I worked closely on a number of technical subjects including my attempt to computerize charts that he later published in the *Journal of Business* and was later the basis for Arthur Merrill's book, *Filtered Waves*, on chart patterns in the market averages.

The Evidence

In the next three chapters, I explain a recent study I performed that investigated the profit value of three different stock selection techniques. I looked at relative price-to-sales for the valuation method, relative quarterly reported earnings growth for the growth method, and relative price strength for a technical method. The peculiarities of each are shown as I review the outcome of the experiments.

I used data from the U. S. stock market from 1998 through 2006. This sample includes a major stock market decline and subsequent rise. To measure the subsequent performance of each method, I used relative strength performance of the selection methods over each type of background market up and down as well as over the entire period. The study looked at the prices of 8,073 stocks and 290,594 weekly observations, a large enough number to assure statistical significance. Each stock was recorded weekly with its current price and the three relative ratios (value, growth, and price strength), as well as the subsequent relative price strength percentile for 3 months, 6 months, and 12 months ahead.

Relative performance was calculated using the relative strength percentile calculation (for details on the calculation see Chapter 9, "Relative Price Strength Selection") to eliminate the effect of the market on the price performance. In a rising market, the strongest stocks will naturally have the best percentage performance, and in a declining market, the strongest stocks will have poor percentage performance even though they still perform better than their weaker competitors do. If I took the actual percentage performance rather than the relative performance, the stronger stocks' aggregated performance would be overly weighted to periods of market rise. Because I wanted to test the method and not the market, the performance was measured relative to the market.

Summary

Any method you use to invest must make sense and be tested. I have looked at the three principle ways of analyzing stocks to find what methods I believe are the best. The basic concept I found first is to eliminate market action in selecting stocks by using relative data rather than absolute data. Relative data becomes independent of the market and gives a better picture of how a stock is performing technically and fundamentally against all other stocks. I am looking for the best stocks and leaving the market direction to portfolio management. The three principle ways that analysts look at stocks are value, growth, and price. In the following chapters I show you the tests of these relative methods and how I have determined the trigger points for buying and selling. Various statistical figures are shown on each performance chart for those who have enough knowledge of statistics to use for closer evaluation of each result. The following three chapters can be complex reading and an understanding of them is not necessary to invest using the relative method. They describe the tests performed on the three methods (price-to-sales, reported earnings growth, and price strength) in detail and show how the trigger points were derived. If your eyes begin to gloss over with the details, simply look at the summary table of trigger points at the end of each chapter and continue to Chapter 10, "Putting It Together."

CHAPTER 7

VALUE SELECTION

The method I use to value each stock is the *price-to-sales ratio*. This ratio is simply the ratio between the stock's weekly closing price and the last four quarters of reported sales for the company. The sales first are divided by the number of shares outstanding to create the price-per-sales per share. In the tests, I calculated this ratio for every stock for every week over the period 1998 through 2006. All stocks were sorted by their price-to-sales ratio; then they were ranked in percentiles based on 99 being the highest price-to-sales ratio to zero, the lowest. Each stock's relative price performance percentile was then recorded for the following 3-, 6-, and 12-month periods. This way I knew for any relative price-to-sales percentile what its relative price performance was 3, 6, and 12 months later and could collect these figures by percentile to give an estimate of what the effect of relative price-to-sales had on the future relative price performance of stocks.

I use price-to-sales as a measure of value for two reasons. It was found by James O'Shaughnessy (*What Works on Wall Street*) to be the best relationship to future performance, and because sales numbers are the least likely to be manipulated by management. Price-to-sales seems to be the most easily considered, readily available, and accurate calculation of relative value.

Description of Performance Charts

Figure 7.1 is an example of the performance charts used in this chapter and the following two chapters.

The horizontal axis marked from 2 to 97 gives the collective relative rankings, by percentile, for each stock's relative price-to-sales ratio. The lowest percentiles represent those stocks with the lowest relative price-to-sales valuations, and the high numbers on the right are those stocks with high valuations.

- The vertical axis on the left side of the chart represents the performance ranking for each level of relative price-to-sales over a period of 3, 6, or 12 months. The curved line represents where relative performance and price-to-sales percentile intersected in the tests. In Figure 7.1, you can deduce what relative price-to-sales ratios resulted in what relative performance. If you draw a line directly up from the price-to-sales percentile of 97, for example, it intersects the curved line at a relative performance of 40.8. This is below the 50th percentile average performance for the market. A performance of 50 is the midpoint and is, thus, the average for the overall market performance. Any part of the curved line above that horizontal performance percentile 50 level suggests that the corresponding price-to-sales percentiles outperformed the market, and that any part below the 50 performance level implied future underperformance.

- The curved line on the chart represents reality. The straight line is the "best fit" line through the curved line and represents the ideal. It is important to look at the direction of the straight line (in Figure 7.1, the direction is downward from left to right) to see if the relationship between valuation and subsequent performance is direct or inverse. If the slope is upward to the right, the selection criteria are directly related to later relative performance. The higher the percentile figures, the better the performance. In Figure 7.1, the line is headed downward. This indicates that the relationship between the selection criteria (relative price-to-sales ratio percentile) is inversely related to relative performance. As the value percentile increases, future performance decreases. Therefore, for price-to-sales percentiles, lower is better.

Current Relative Price-to-Sales and Relative Price Strength Three Months Ahead

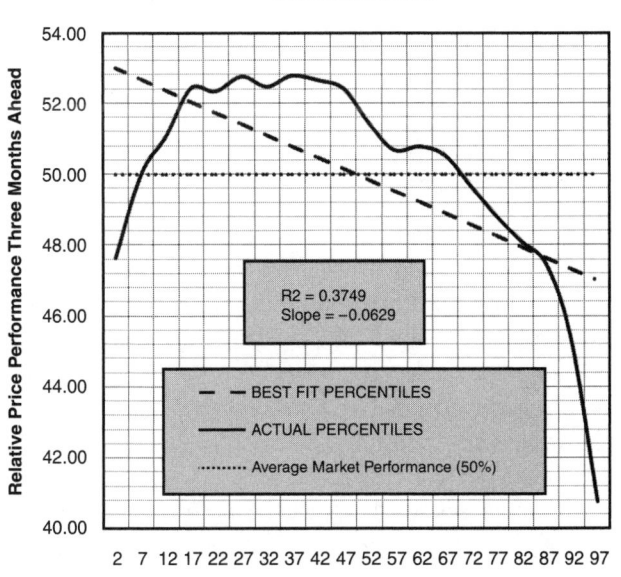

$R^2 = 0.3749$
Slope $= -0.0629$

— — BEST FIT PERCENTILES
——— ACTUAL PERCENTILES
········· Average Market Performance (50%)

Current Relative Price-to-Sales Percentile

Figure 7.1
Relative value percentile versus relative price performance percentile after three months

It is also important to look at the steepness of the straight line. The steeper it is, the better is the relationship. "Steep" is measured by the "slope" number in the table and is independent of the direction of the line. The higher the slope number, the steeper and, thus, better the relationship. It can be steep upward or downward. A negative slope means that the relationship is inverse. In later charts on relative earnings growth and price performance, you will see a direct relationship that has a positive slope number.

- Finally, you want to know how well the data "fits" the straight line. In Figure 7.1, an eyeball inspection indicates a relatively close fit between the curved line and the straight line from relative price-to-sales percentiles 17 to 87. At high rankings, the curved line deviates sharply downward from the straight line, indicating a poor fit at those levels. The R2 number in the table is a mathematical measure of fit and ranges between 0 and 1.0 where 0 is no fit and 1.00 is a perfect fit. The R2 in Figure 7.1 is 0.3749, a decent fit, but not as desirable as a fit above 0.70, which is preferred. Perfection is almost never reached.

The results of this specific test are that the best three-month relative performance resulted from price-to-sales percentiles above the straight line and the 50 level at or near the peaks in the curved line at 27 and 37. When the curve rises above the 50 performance percentile, especially above the straight line, a buy trigger is established, and when the curved line declines through the 50 level, a sell trigger is identified. You should look, therefore, for stocks to purchase in the 17 and 47 range, including 10 points on either side of the peaks because they have the best chance of outperforming the market over the following three months.

Performance Three Months Ahead

In relative price-to-sales ratio percentiles, low numbers are favorable until they reach below seven. The lower the assessment the market makes of a stock, presumably the less the capital risk. Naturally, you want stocks that will perform with minimal risk. The test over three months shows that relatively low price-to-sales percentiles resulted in above-average performance. As relative valuation advanced, the relative price performance deteriorated. The straight line through the results pointed downward and to the right on the chart, and the actual figures fit closely to that line. As Figure 7.1 shows, the belief that undervalued stocks are good buys proved true.

Two percentile groupings show deviations from that straight line that could be important. For the lowest relative price-to-sales percentiles, those below seven, the curved line heads downward to the left. This deviation from the straight line indicates that stocks with ultra-low relative valuations have poor performance. Poor performance at these levels can only mean that when stock prices reach low levels of valuation, there is likely a strong reason for their failure to perform in the immediate three months ahead. These stocks have something wrong with them and cannot bounce back with favorable future performance. As an investor, you can feel assured that low valuations are generally favorable for you to profit, but that ultra-low valuations can be harmful to your investment performance.

The other deviation from the straight line occurs at high levels of relative valuation. These are stocks trading at excessively high price-to-sales ratios, relative to all others, and as the chart shows are even more susceptible to a potential failure in performance over three months. The curved line declines even more sharply above the relative price-to-sales 87th percentile, and at the 99th percentile, it shows the worse performance three months out of any relative valuation. If you own a stock with this high of a relative valuation, your profit odds will improve if you sell it.

In this chart, the curved line crosses below the 50th relative performance percentile when relative price-to-sales reach the 72nd percentile. Any stock above the 72nd relative price-to-sales percentile is more likely to fail than to profit. It is the ideal trigger to a sell any stock in a portfolio. In addition, relative price performance rapidly deteriorates at a price-to-sales percentile of 7 or less. A decline below this level is a second sell trigger.

On the buy side, it appears that the range between the 17th and 47th percentile is the best area to select stocks. This is where the relative price performance three months ahead is substantially above the market average.

Performance Six Months Ahead

Performance more than six months ahead improves using relative price-to-sales. Figure 7.2 shows how well the results fit a straight line and how much steeper the slope of that line is compared to the three-month results.

The relationship between relative price-to-sales to performance over six months is stronger than over the three-month outcome. The downward slope of the line is steeper and the line fits the data better.

In the three-month test, the slope number was −0.0629. In the current test of performance six months in the future, the slope number is −0.0940, almost 50 percent steeper. This suggests that when using relative price-to-sales, it works better for six-month performance. Should the slope number be near zero, we would have an indication that there was no relationship at all between valuation and later price performance. Fortunately, you can see that there is a strong correlation between the two figures.

Current Relative Price-to-Sales and Relative Price Strength Six Months Ahead

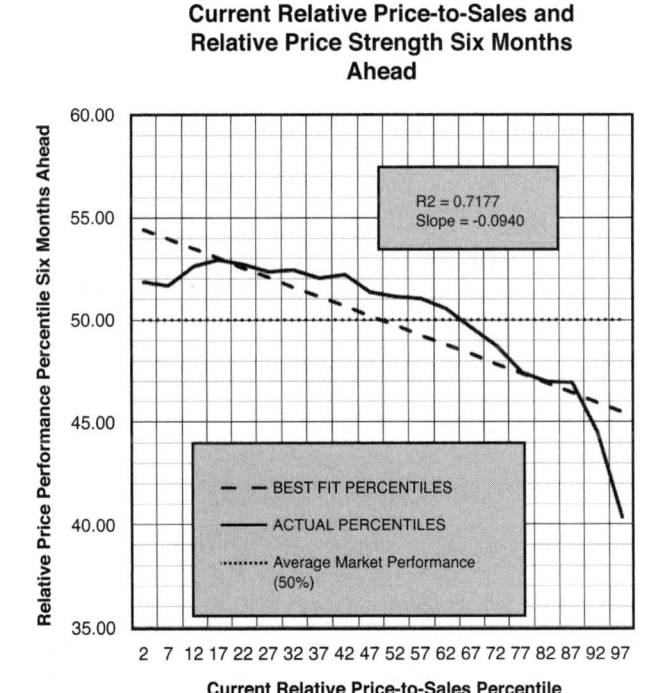

[Chart: Relative Price Performance Percentile Six Months Ahead (y-axis, 35.00 to 60.00) versus Current Relative Price-to-Sales Percentile (x-axis, 2 to 97). $R^2 = 0.7177$, Slope = -0.0940. Legend: Best Fit Percentiles, Actual Percentiles, Average Market Performance (50%).]

Figure 7.2
Relative value percentile versus relative price performance percentile after six months

As mentioned earlier, how close the results fit a straight line is measured by R2, with a perfect, but unlikely, fit R2 equal to 1.0000 and no fit equal to 0. As for fit to the six-month line in Figure 7.2, the R2 is 0.7177, a high reading that indicates the relationship between relative price-to-sales and relative price performance out six months is strong. Any figure above 0.70 is excellent. In Figure 7.2, the high portion of the actual figures in the low valuation area has flattened and is above the 50 relative performance percentile for the entire period. This is different from Figure 7.1, the three-month performance chart, where the low valuations show below-average relative performance. It shows that while low valuations will be nonproductive over three months, their performance improves over six months. I would still be wary, however, of choosing stocks with ultra-low valuations because I don't want to have to live through the three-month period of possible low performance. On the right end of the straight line, the actual numbers nose dive just as they did in the three-month test. There is little question, then, that over both the three- and six-month periods, stocks with high relative price-to-sales ratios tend to underperform all other stocks.

Using relative price-to-sales percentiles, you should consider buying only stocks with close to the peaks in the curved line at 17 and 32. These buy points are ideal, and stocks with value percentiles between 12 and 42 can also be considered. These triggers are similar to those selected for the three-month test and should be considered the standard for any purchases.

On the sell side, you certainly don't want to own and should sell any stock with a relative price-to-sales percentile greater than 67 where the curved line crosses below the 50th percentile ranking of performance. Below that level you can expect underperformance six months out. The three-month results showed the optimal selling point was when the stock's valuation percentile ranking reached as high as 72. Somewhere above the 67 price-to-sales percentile is the level where the stock is too highly valued and is the best zone in which to sell stocks.

Performance Twelve Months Ahead

In Figure 7.3, for the 12-month performance of selecting stocks based on relative price-to-sales, the relationship has changed considerably. The straight line is now practically flat; its slope is a measly 0.0051. This means there is little or no relationship between the relative price-to-sales percentile of a stock and its performance ranking 12 months later. Thus, relative valuation is a useless selection criterion out that far in the future.

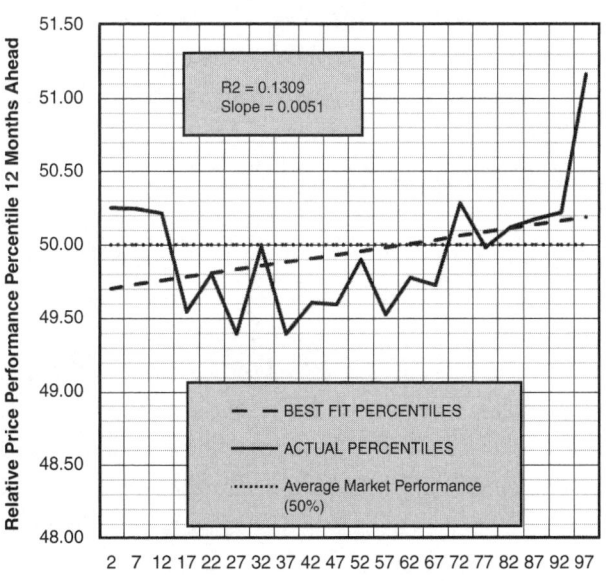

Current Relative Price-to-Sales and Relative Price Strength 12 Months Ahead

$R^2 = 0.1309$
Slope = 0.0051

— — BEST FIT PERCENTILES
——— ACTUAL PERCENTILES
········ Average Market Performance (50%)

Current Relative Price-to-Sales Percentile

Figure 7.3
Relative price-to-sales percentile versus relative price performance percentile after 12 months

Advancing and Declining Background Market

There is not much question that the direction of the overall stock market has important effects on the performance of individual stocks. For one thing, strong stocks tend to have better absolute price advances in rising stock markets versus declining markets. This is why I decided to look at stocks' relative performances rather than their percentage returns. Relative returns for stocks in a bull market would be different during a bear-market period. To alleviate this bias toward market direction, I used the relative price strength rankings. It is interesting to see how each selection method behaves in different markets. For this reason, I decided to break the entire period of study into two components of roughly the same length—one being a bull market and the other a bear market—to see just how these different market directions affected the results of each selection method.

In Figure 7.4, market direction is defined by how it is positioned versus a 12-month simple moving average of the Dow Jones Industrial Average. This is an easy method of determining whether the market is in a bull (advancing) phase or a bear (declining) phase. This method is not a scientific procedure for determining the long-term direction of the market and should not be used necessarily in the future. For the period from 2000 to 2007, however, it gives a realistic assessment of the general market direction and is, therefore, suitable for my use in these tests.

When the Standard & Poor's Index monthly close was above its 12-month moving average (roughly April 2003 to April 2007), I defined the background market as "advancing." When the monthly index close was below its 12-month moving average (roughly September 2000 through March 2003), I defined the background market as "declining." I then looked at the different relative rankings and their subsequent performance rankings during each market direction to see how the background market direction might have influenced the earlier results for the entire period of up and down markets. I used the three-month future performance rankings to minimize the effects of market reversals.

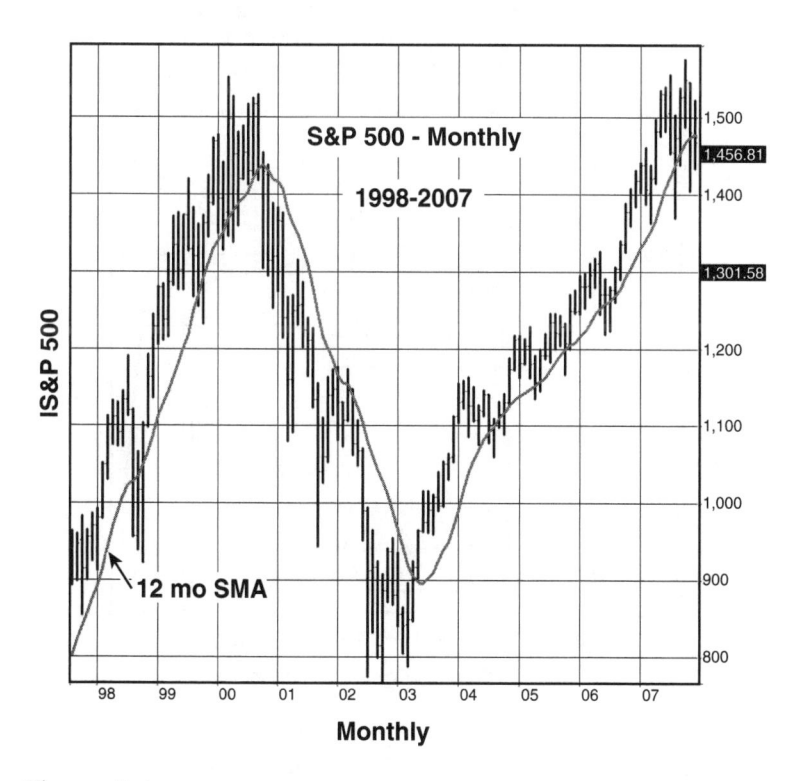

Figure 7.4
Advancing stock market and declining stock market—monthly with 12-month simple moving average (1998 to 2007)

Compare Figure 7.5 with Figure 7.1. The slope of the best-fit line is still downward, indicating the expected inverse relationship to performance, but the slope of that line is not as steep as earlier (–0.02 versus –0.06). The relationship, therefore, is one-third as strong as for all markets. Because the relationship is so weak in an advancing market, the relationship must be especially strong in a declining market.

Current Relative Price-to-Sales and Relative Price Strength Three Months Ahead in a Rising Stock Market

$R^2 = 0.1291$
Slope = -0.0243

– – BEST FIT PERCENTILES
—— ACTUAL PERCENTILES
·········· Average Market Performance (50%)

Current Price-to-Sales Percentile

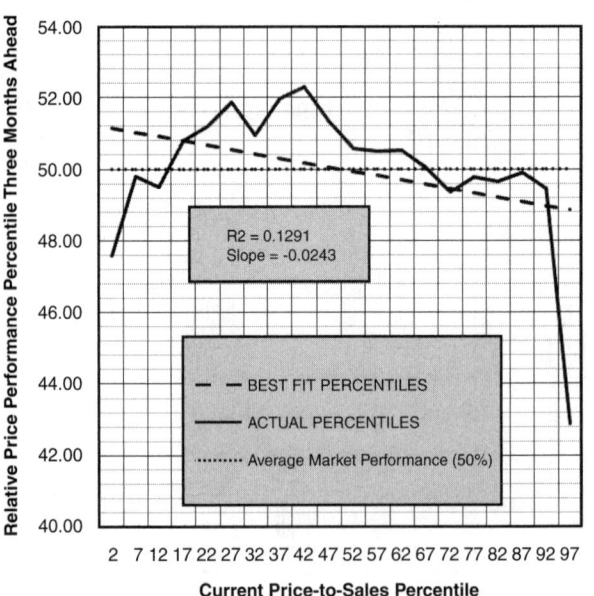

Figure 7.5
Relative value percentile versus relative price performance percentile—after three months in an advancing stock market

The earlier chart in Figure 7.1 suggested that the optimal price-to-sales percentile for purchases of stock lies between the

Value Selection

17th and 42nd. These are levels similar to those in an advancing market.

Similar to the earlier charts of performance from selecting stocks on relative price-to-sales, the range above the percentile 92 shows terrible future performance in an advancing market. Indeed, relative performance declines below average when the relative valuation exceeds the percentile 67. In earlier tests without market direction, percentile 72 was also the best cut-off for selling stocks in a portfolio.

Relative Price-to-Sales Percentile During a Declining Market After Three Months

During a declining background stock market, the straight-line correlation between relative valuation and stock performance three months later (see Figure 7.6) bears an exaggerated resemblance to Figure 7.1 of the relationship during the entire period irrespective of market direction. The straight line is headed steeply downward to the right, creating a good inverse correlation. As the valuation rankings advanced, the future performance declined, just as common sense would suggest. The slope of the best-fit line was four times that of the line during an advancing market and about 25 percent greater than for the entire period of difficulties in the market. Relative valuation is a more important selection criterion during a declining market—you want to buy stocks then.

As in Figure 7.1, Figure 7.6 shows how stocks with ultra-low relative valuation rankings are not good investments during bear markets. Bankruptcy or future problems are discounted in the price, and historically, they were a poor bet. However, they were not as poor a bet as those stocks with extraordinarily high value rankings. Again, these were the worst performers over the following three months.

Current Relative Price-to-Sales and Relative Price Strength Three Months Ahead in a Declining Market

[Chart: R2 = 0.4836, Slope = −0.0827; x-axis: Current Relative Price-to-Sales Percentile; y-axis: Relative Price Performance Percentile Three Months Ahead; legend: BEST FIT PERCENTILES, ACTUAL PERCENTILES, Average Market Performance (50%)]

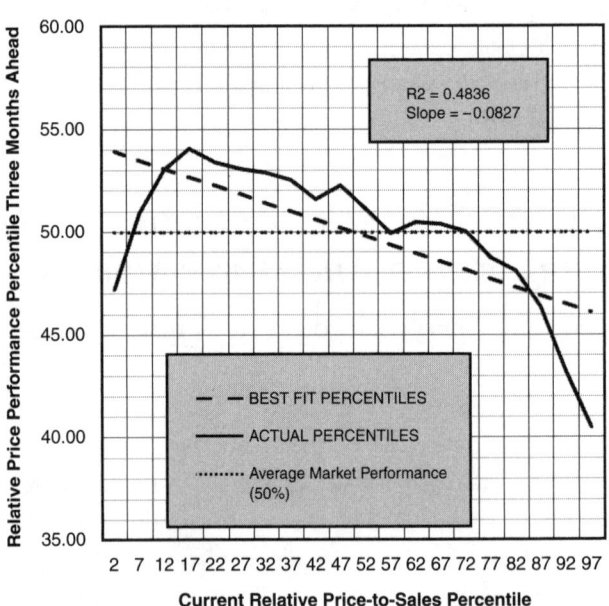

Figure 7.6
Relative value percentile versus relative price performance percentile over three months in a declining stock market

Assuming you know you are in a bear market, the best buying valuation rankings are between the 17th and 27nd percentile, with the optimal around the 17th percentile. Selling should occur when the valuation ranking reaches above the 57th percentile or below the 7th percentile.

Summary

Generally, in the progression from lower relative price-to-sales percentile rankings to higher, the performance rankings of stocks deteriorated over the periods of three and six months. This relationship disappeared for periods out to 12 months. Remember that in Dreman's study of analysts' earnings projections, he found that projections a year ahead were almost useless—only one in 170 analysts were correct within 5 percent. This study also suggests performance out a year is almost impossible to predict even with known data. Dreman's data used analyst predictions, and my data uses actual reported data. Neither seems to be useful out as far as 12 months. I believe there is no way to anticipate stock prices out a year, and that buying stocks for long-term capital gain and for tax reasons is a futile exercise. These studies don't show that such a goal is impossible, only that it is unrealistic to assume when buying a stock. In many cases, a stock is bought on anticipation of a short-term gain, 3 months, for example, and turns out to maintain its excellent relative characteristics for more than 1 year, in which case, if you own it, you are lucky. However, to assume that performance beyond the range of three to six months is predictable to any extent is dangerous because you might end up holding stocks for 12 months just to realize the benefit of tax treatment but lose capital because the relative ranking changes the odds of continued profit. In the following chapters on reported earnings growth and relative price strength, all the rankings are useless for performance out 12 months. This suggests to me that investment should *not* be focused on such a long outlook but instead should begin with a shorter, more predictable outlook and continue as long as the rankings remain favorable. A portfolio must be monitored at intervals considerably less than a year, as often as each week or month at the longest, for continued success and maximum gains.

TABLE 7.1
Best Trigger Levels for Relative Price-to-Sales Percentile Ranking

Trigger	Relative Percentile Ranking
Best Buy Zone	17–42
Best Sell Zone	Greater than 67 and less than 7

The percentiles that produced the best future performance in stocks using the relative price-to-sales method are between 17 and 42. Superior performance occurred within this range out three and six months in both advancing and declining markets. On the sell side, there are two brackets: A stock showing price-to-sales percentiles less than 7 or greater than 67 should be sold. I am not emphasizing short sales in this book, but certainly the tests have shown that any stock with a valuation percentile ranking above 90 could be considered, if it is confirmed by other information, for short selling. I do not advocate short selling because capital risks are too high for the average investor.

CHAPTER 8

RELATIVE REPORTED EARNINGS GROWTH SELECTION

Predicted earnings for companies are generally inadequate out to a year and beyond. For this reason, I use only reported earnings, hoping that the company reporting them is not taking too much leeway. I have read numerous studies on earnings and learned how popular the use of earnings can be for investors. Unfortunately, few have studied whether earnings reports or projections—although they intuitively sound like a reason for investment—have actually faired in the real world. The anticipated earnings are usually wrong and, indeed, one commentator stated that an investor is better off using reported earnings than those anticipated by security analysts. That is precisely what I do. I use only reported earnings. This doesn't mean that reported earnings are error-free. Most analysts take reported earnings as a base and calculate forward. One of my favorite courses at Wharton was on analyzing financial statements to see how corporations could fudge the numbers using numerous tricks to make their reported earnings look better. It was a sad tale, but it was certainly eye-opening. We must be careful with reported earnings and predicted earnings because they also may be suspect. For example, Enron management was faking the numbers and causing reputable analysts to make serious errors in recommendations for the stock. There is not much we can do about earnings accuracy except to be aware that they may not be completely truthful. This confidence failure demonstrates the importance of relying on reputable management and auditors to reduce the likelihood of accounting deception.

To calculate the reported earnings relative rankings for each stock, I take the last four quarters of reported operating earnings for each company and calculate a ratio of this total to the four-quarter total one quarter earlier. Taking only operating earnings means I eliminate special charges or adjustments to earnings (such as the result of a merger or back adjustments for taxes) to get just the core operating earnings. Taking the reported quarterly earnings over a full four quarters reduces the effect of seasonality that can occur in most businesses. The earnings reported each quarter are the quickest set of readings available. Obviously, much can happen to a company within a quarter, and the stock price may adjust before the next quarterly earnings report. For example, the recent write-offs in bank loan portfolios will not be reflected in the banks' earnings until the end of their fiscal quarter. Thus, this reported earnings method is limited in the timeliness of the information. This was also a problem in using the price-to-sales ratio earlier. Sales are reported on a quarterly basis as well, but I still found the information useful for selecting stocks.

The ratio of the most recent four quarters earnings per share to the four quarters one quarter earlier is calculated for each stock with positive earnings, and the entire list is then ranked into percentiles from 99 (the best) to zero (the worst). Those stocks with negative earnings over either four-quarter period are eliminated from the earnings list. As in the study of the price-to-sales ratio percentile rankings, I look at the 3-, 6-, and 12-month results in the relative stock price percentile rankings to see if a valid relationship exists. Logically, it should be directly correlated;

that is, higher earnings growth should produce higher relative price performance over each measured period. This means that Figure 8.1 should show a positive slope between relative earnings growth percentiles and stock relative performance.

Current Relative Earnings Growth Percentile versus Relative Price Performance Three Months Ahead

R2 = 0.3464
Slope = 0.342

- - BEST FIT PERCENTILES
— ACTUAL PERCENTILES
······ Average Market Performance (50%)

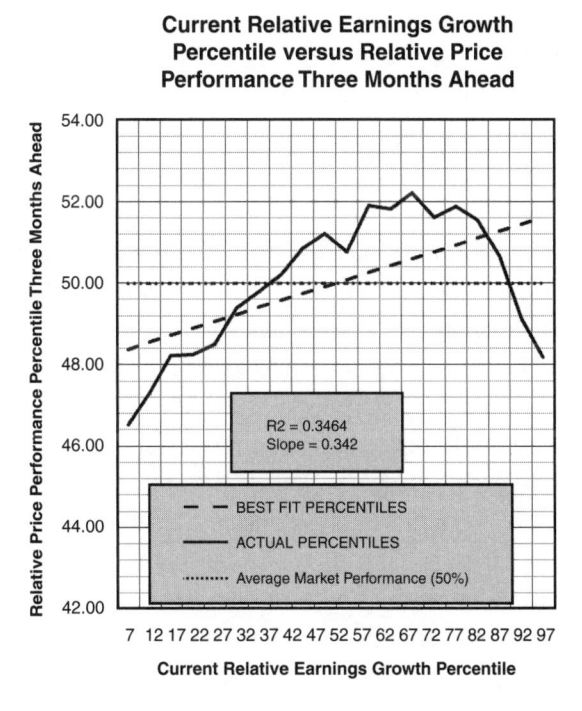

Figure 8.1
Relative earnings growth percentile versus relative price performance after three months

In Figure 8.1, as expected, the slope of the results is positive, moving upward to the right. There is a direct correlation between reported earnings growth and subsequent relative stock price performance. The overall slope, however, is not as large as the three-month results for relative price-to-sales; indeed, it is only half the slope of the relative value method in the last chapter. Reported earnings growth might not be useful selection criteria for finding stocks. However, if you eliminate the downward slope of the actual figures that occur on the extreme right side, the overall slope of the remaining relative earnings growth rankings improves, but there are ominous deviations from the straight line. At the end of the line on the right, as earnings growth improves to its highest levels, the relative performance drops off and actually declines below the market average at the ultra-high levels of earnings growth in the top-ten percentiles. This is quite strange. I would think that the higher the earnings growth, the higher the performance, but for some odd reason, the ultra-high numbers move against the trend. This might have to do with the high earnings being overly expected or that ultra-high earnings are not supportable over time and lead to a price decline. *The Economist* (April 12, 2008, pp. 83) says that Westamarka Bancorporation of California was criticized for not participating in the high-yielding property loans. Its president stated, "If it grows too fast, it's a weed." This observation seems to also apply to reported earnings. The high-end decline is not an expected result for most investors and analysts and brings into question whether reported earnings should be used at all.

If you persist in using relative reported earnings as a selection technique, however, you must keep away from those stocks showing earnings rankings above earnings percentile 92. This is a little ironic because, as you will see in Chapter 10, "Putting It Together," I have used these high levels of relative earnings in a successful model for the last 30 years. Perhaps I must adjust that model.

Because the slope is upward, I know that there is at least a positive relationship between earnings growth and performance, but it appears that the better performance only occurs between the earnings growth percentiles of 42 to 87 before it drops off sharply. Performance is below average for earnings with rankings less than 37 and greater than 92. These bounds could be used as sell triggers.

Current Relative Earnings Growth Percentile and Relative Price Strength Percentile Six Months Ahead

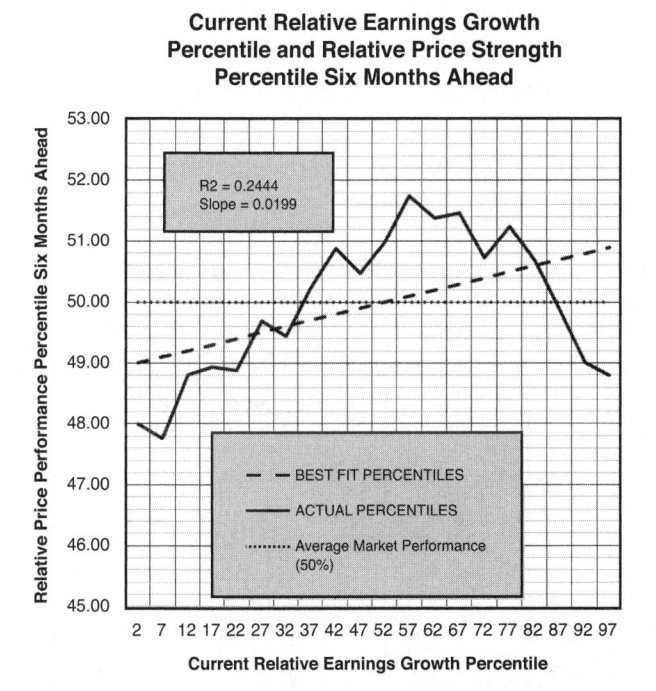

Figure 8.2
Relative earnings growth percentile versus relative price performance percentile ahead six months

In Figure 8.2, the line showing the relation between the earnings growth percentile and the subsequent performance over six months is similar to the line from the three-month chart but at the higher growth percentiles, the performance remains above the market average. The slope of the best-fit line (0.0199) is only about 60 percent that of the three-month slope (0.0342) and is less consistent. This decline in slope suggests that the relationship between earnings and performance is becoming even less significant as you look out in time. The R2 figure, a measure of fitness to the line, is 0.2444 versus 0.3464 for the three-month results. This means that the lower slope is even less representative of the actual numbers and that the relationship between earnings and performance is questionable. This lack of correlation and failure to act intuitively at high levels again raises the suspicion that relative earnings growth may not be a good selection criterion.

Current Relative Earnings Growth Percentile and Relative Price Strength Percentile 12 Months Ahead

$R2 = 0.0635$
Slope = 0.020

— — BEST FIT PERCENTILES
—— ACTUAL PERCENTILES
········ Average Market Performance (50%)

Current Relative Earnings Growth Percentile

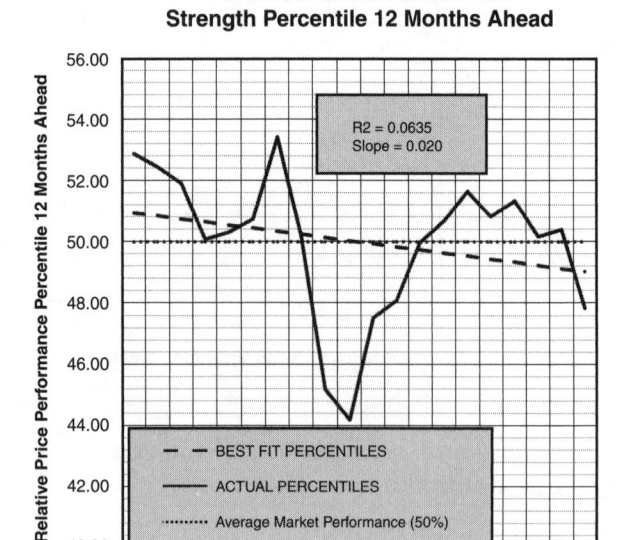

Figure 8.3
Relative earnings growth percentile versus relative price strength percentile after 12 months

Relative Reported Earnings Growth Selection

Figure 8.3 shows that for performance 12 months ahead, the relative ranking of earnings growth had little or no effect on the performance of a stock. The fit to the line is erratic and the direction of the line is downward, suggesting that higher earnings growth had a slightly negative influence on price performance. This is not what should be expected but bolsters my earlier argument that investing for 12 months or more is pointless. Because the statistical measures are weak, I discount earnings growth completely in looking at stock performance 12 months out.

Predictably, a rising market helps stocks that are reporting above-average relative earnings growth. Figure 8.4 shows an ideal relationship between relative earnings growth and relative performance three months ahead. The slope of the line (0.07) is the highest of any slope for earnings growth and comes close to the highest slope numbers for relative price-to-sales. The chart suggests that during advancing markets relative earnings is an effective method of selecting stocks. Even when the top end at the high levels of earnings growth percentiles begins to drop off, the performance numbers remain at a high level of relative performance.

Using relative reported earnings growth during a bull market, the 57th percentile and above gives above-average performance out three months. The time to sell is when the earnings percentile ranking declines below 52. Make sure you are in a bull market, however. The results for a bear market are indecipherable.

As Figure 8.5 shows, in a declining stock market, earnings growth is an unreliable selection method. Whenever the best-fit line is flat, it indicates that there is no relationship between the variables. In Figure 8.5, the best-fit line is flat, about as flat as can be. Thus, in a declining market, the chart concludes that

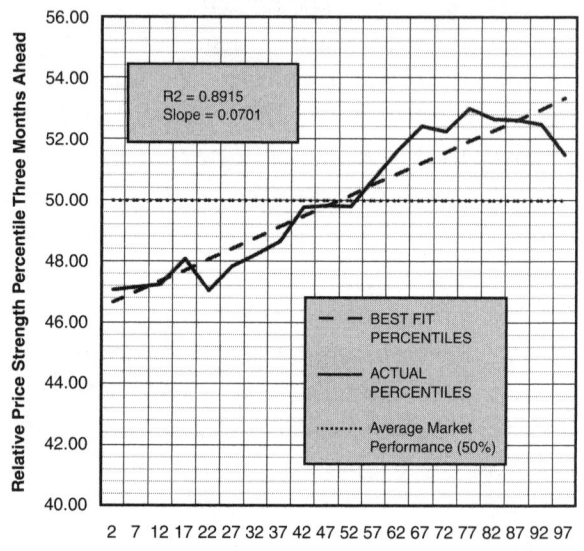

Current Relative Earnings Growth and Relative Price Strength in a Rising Stock Market Three Months Ahead

$R2 = 0.8915$
Slope = 0.0701

- - - BEST FIT PERCENTILES
—— ACTUAL PERCENTILES
······ Average Market Performance (50%)

Figure 8.4
Relative earnings growth percentile versus relative price strength percentile in an advancing stock market after three months

there is no relationship between relative reported earnings growth and performance three months later. Picking a stock with any earnings growth will not produce profitable investments during a declining market, and those stocks with especially high or low earnings growth will perform poorly. This figure combined with Figure 8.4 shows that the only way to use relative earnings growth profitably is to do so *only during a bull market*. By adding this requirement, your investment decisions must include an additional assessment about market direction.

Current Relative Earnings Growth Percentile and Relative Price Strength Percentile in a Declining Market Three Months Ahead

R2 = 0.0004
Slope = -0.0014

- - BEST FIT PERCENTILES
—— ACTUAL PERCENTILES

Current Relative Earnings Growth Percentiles

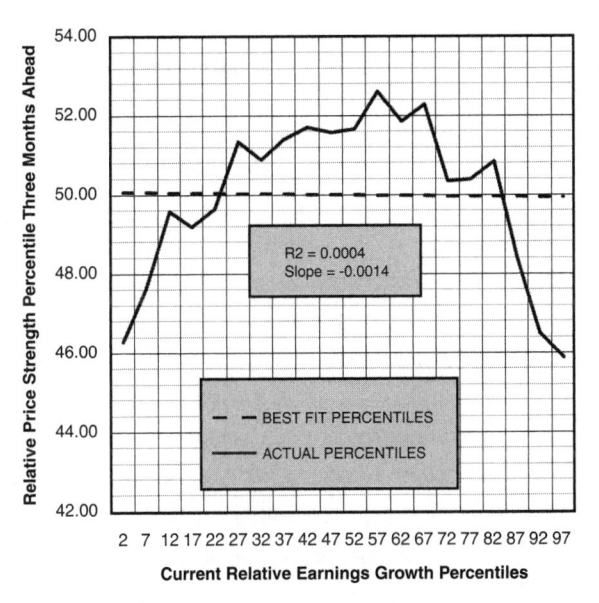

Figure 8.5
Relative earnings growth percentile versus relative price strength percentile in a declining market after three months

Because it is not always easy to determine the longer-term direction of the general market, the earnings growth method is unreliable.

Summary

The best rankings for buying and selling stocks based on relative reported earnings percentiles are in Table 8.1. Please note that the only time these triggers are useful is in a bull market. Otherwise, they are useless.

TABLE 8.1
Best Trigger Levels for Relative Reported Earnings Growth Percentile Ranking

Trigger	Relative Percentile Ranking
Best Buy Zone (only during an advancing market)	57 and above (the higher the better)
Best Sell Zone (only during an advancing market)	Below 52

In all the preceding tests, the price performance fell off at the higher levels of earnings growth, a counterintuitive result. During a declining stock market, the earnings growth percentile has no value at all, requiring that the investor know the direction of the market. The doubt created by the results in this test is enough for me to eliminate the earnings growth technique as being untrustworthy and potentially harmful.

I have used relative reported earnings growth in creating earlier models of stock selection that have been profitable, but I didn't test the relationship between high growth in earnings and performance results 30 years ago when I first began these studies. The relationship was assumed, just as it is today in many investment houses. This assumption that earnings growth, especially exceptional earnings growth, is a desirable factor for selecting stocks is now somewhat tainted. Indeed, my models actually increase in performance once the earnings growth factor is eliminated.

CHAPTER 9

RELATIVE PRICE STRENGTH SELECTION

The most reliable technique for selecting stocks is relative price strength. There are many ways of calculating relative price strength and some are publicly available. Most of the popular data suppliers use their own proprietary method and refuse to divulge the calculation details. *Investors' Business Daily* is one that comes to mind. On the other hand, *Value Line* published its calculation of relative price strength as "dividing the stock's latest ten-week average relative price by its 52-week average relative price." You are better off locating a data supplier that will calculate relative price strength as outlined here or purchase raw data and calculate the ratios and rankings yourself. The tests in this chapter use a specific method that is available from various recommended data and software vendors (see Chapter 11, "Selecting and Deleting Stocks").

Relative Strength Calculations

Few portfolio managers at the time of Levy's article accepted his concept of relative strength (see Chapter 6, "Meeting the Relatives"). It lay dormant, at least in academia, for almost 30 years. Then, in 1998, UCLA professors (at the time of their article) Narisimhan Jegadeesh and Sheridan Titman performed a far simpler test using just the percentage changes in stock prices over 3 to 12 month periods. Measuring the subsequent performance of each stock, categorized by their earlier percentage change, they found a direct, statistically significant correlation between relative price change and later price performance up to 12 months later. The most consistent period for defining the initial relative strength was six months. They found the peak in performance occurred roughly seven months out with monthly returns dropping off and becoming negative during the following two years. The cumulative return turned negative after the first 11 months. Since that article, others in academia have searched in other countries and found similar results, and in 2001, Jegadeesh and Titman followed up their study and demonstrated the relationship still to be true.

Relative strength seems to work in selecting profitable stocks at least over specific periods. It tends not to work over short periods or for periods longer than a year.

I use a method similar to the Levy method. Each week, I calculate the ratio of the current weekly closing price to the 26-week moving average (around 126 trading days versus Levy's 131 days) of closing prices so that I need only look at the results once a week. I rank the entire list in percentiles with 99 as the highest and zero as the lowest. I test just as I do for relative performance over the subsequent periods of 3, 6, and 12 months. The ratio calculation is sensitive to shorter-term price changes because price is the numerator. The moving average in the denominator tends to keep the ratio advancing or declining with the stock's trend and when compared to changes in the current prices, gives early warnings of changes in trend.

Relative Price Strength Selection

When I presented the results in a meeting at the University of Colorado, several professors questioned the use of the same calculation for performance as that for relative price strength. Their concern was focused on the three-month performance using the relative performance ranking. Because the relative strength calculation included three months of the original calculation, they speculated that the calculations overlapped and the performance results would be tainted. This is partially true. Using the relative strength rankings out six months would not affect the six-month results by the time they were calculated; all the original six months of data had passed and would not overlap. For three months there is an overlap. My counter argument was that the overlap occurs in a moving average in the performance ratio denominator, which has been smoothed out to some extent over half the period. On the other hand, the numerator (the price) can oscillate substantially over the three-month interval and would have little to do with the six-month results. The numerator has more to do with changes in the ratio than the slow-moving denominator. In conclusion, the overlapping should have a minimal effect on the results.

The result from fitting the calculations of relative price strength ranking to price strength rankings three months ahead is the best-fit line seen of any of the previous tests in this book. The slope is upward (0.326), more than five times steeper than the relative valuation method and 9.5 times steeper than the relative earnings growth method. This is counterintuitive to some who believe that low rankings should reverse upward and that high rankings should falter. Nevertheless, the fit is so good and so close that intuition is obviously incorrect. Relative price strength seems to breed more relative strength, and relative weakness breeds further relative weakness. This implies that you are better off buying a stock that is trading at its high than buying one that is trading at its low, contrary to the human natural bias toward a bargain. Stocks with low relative price-to-sales outperform the market in the relative value tests above, and strong stocks outperform the market as well. This apparent conflict can be resolved by finding stocks that meet both criteria. Stocks with low valuations and high strength are those coming off price bottoms and showing the first signs of recovery from depleted levels. Logically, aren't these the stocks you want to buy early? Of course.

All results of relative strength above the 47th percentile in the current example have performance greater than the market average three months ahead. The best-fit line hugs the actual figures closely and rises at a steep rate. Steep slopes indicate a higher correlation between the present figure and the future. As for fit, the R2 is 0.8930, well above the 0.700 threshold and more than twice the fit between the results in the price-to-sales and earnings ratio results over three months. It is close to perfect.

Figure 9.1 also shows how to use relative price strength. The best buys are definitely the highest-ranking stocks. The poorest buys are the worst-ranking stocks. The poor performance seems to accelerate as stock becomes even weaker. Buying into a downward trend, attempting to guess when the downward trend will reverse upward, is a dangerous technique and not likely to work. In Wall Street jargon, it is called "catching a falling knife."

Traditionally, I have used relative price strength in the top ten percentiles to time buys. With lower strength rankings, you will find more stocks, but your future performance will be diluted. At the relative strength percentile of 80, the results show average relative performance almost at the 60th percentile, still ten points above average performance. At the relative price strength percentile 97, the resulting percentile is greater than 65. These are the highest performance numbers for any method described in this book. When choosing a stock selection method, there's not much question that relative price strength percentile should be the primary selection criterion and the highest level possible should be the buy trigger. All other techniques should be subordinate to relative price strength.

Current Relative Price Strength Percentile and Relative Price Strength Percentile Three Months Ahead

$R2 = 0.893$
Slope $= 0.326$

— — BEST FIT PERCENTILES
———— ACTUAL PERCENTILES
········ Average Market Performance (50%)

Current Relative Price Strength Percentile

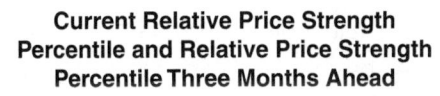

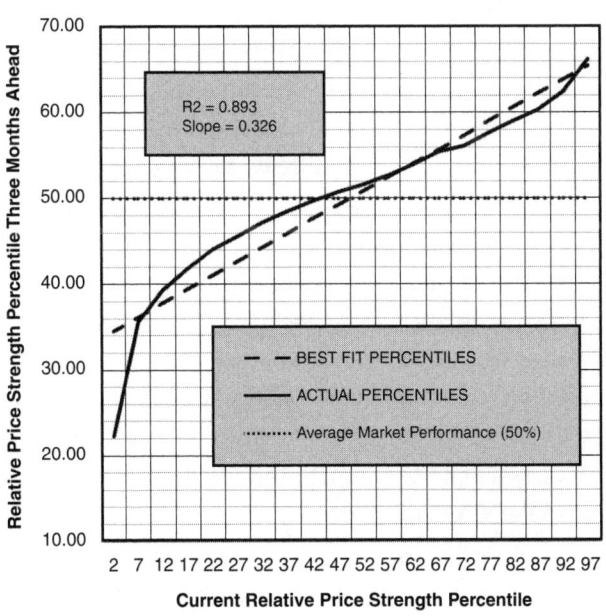

Figure 9.1
Relative strength percentile versus relative strength percentile three months ahead

Over three months, performance turns negative when stocks in the current relative price strength ranks decline below

42. This is the level at which stocks should be eliminated from a list or portfolio.

As performance time lengthens, relative price strength performance gradually deteriorates. The relative price strength percentile, while still showing an excellent correlation (R2 at 0.729, still above the cutoff at 0.700) to future performance six months ahead, loses much of its slope versus three months ahead. It is still considerably better than earnings growth and is slightly behind relative valuation. Any stock having a strength percentile over 37 had a positive performance six months later. The fit to the line is also higher than relative earnings and about the same as relative price-to-sales. The best of the three methods is still relative price strength, with relative price-to-sales second. Relative earnings growth falls far behind as a predictive technique. At the high levels of relative price strength, six-month performance flattens. It is still credible at the 51 to 53 level, but far below the results from the three-month results. The academic argument is that a stock's extra strength is an anomaly in normal price progression and that price will eventually return to normal. Jegadeesh and Titman found the same results. The trend in Figure 9.2 shows this deterioration in average strength and boosts the academic theory. Nevertheless, the anomaly of relative price strength is substantial enough even for a short period to make it a leader in producing profits from past data.

For six-month performance, current strength percentiles ranking between 37 and 99 produce the best results. Stocks below the 32nd percentile fall off steeply in performance. Under no circumstances should a stock ranking below 17 be purchased. At this level and below, the chances of major loss are greater than with any other method.

Current Relative Price Strength and Relative Price Strength Six Months Ahead

[Chart showing Relative Price Strength Percentile Six Months Ahead versus Current Relative Price Strength Percentile, with R2 = 0.7290, Slope = 0.0746. Lines shown: Best Fit Percentiles, Actual Percentiles, Average Market Performance (50%).]

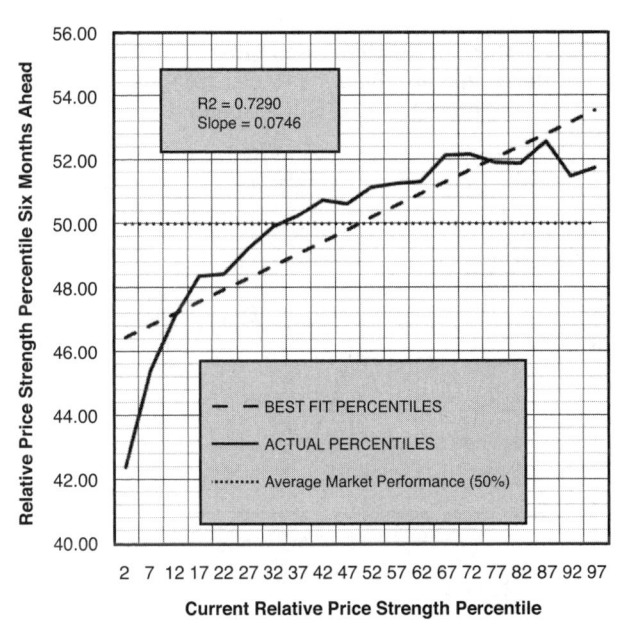

Figure 9.2
Relative price strength percentile versus relative price strength percentile six months ahead

With the possible exception of the high-ranking relative price strength stocks, the relationship between relative strength now and relative strength 12 months later is nonexistent (see Figure 9.3). The correlation is flat, and the best fit is so low that we can assume there is no relationship at all. This is similar to the tests on the other methods of selection over 12 months and reinforces my belief that investing for 12 months is futile. There doesn't seem to be any method that will produce positive results that far in the future. The relative strength concept is the best for shorter periods, but for longer periods, it fails.

Current Relative Price Strength Percentile and Relative Price Strength Percentile 12 Months Ahead

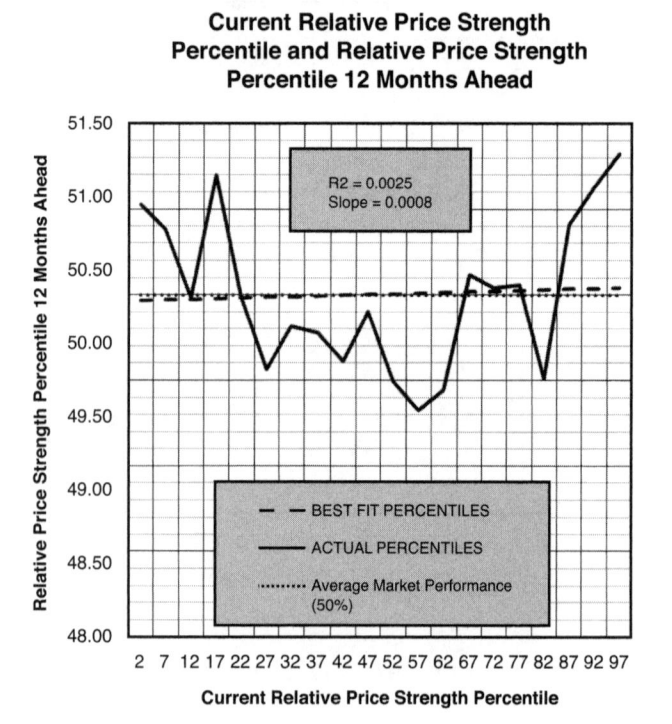

$R^2 = 0.0025$
Slope = 0.0008

- - BEST FIT PERCENTILES
— ACTUAL PERCENTILES
······· Average Market Performance (50%)

Figure 9.3
Relative price strength performance versus relative price strength performance after 12 months

A rising stock market is obviously favorable for relatively strong stocks. The positive slope in Figure 9.4 demonstrates one of the strongest correlations between current stock strength and future stock strength. This relationship is more than 13 times more consistent than using relative price-to-sales ratios and is almost five times better than using relative earnings

Relative Price Strength Selection

growth alone in a rising stock market. In selecting stocks in a rising market, the use of relative stock price strength should be your primary selection criterion.

Current Relative Price Strength Percentile in a Rising Market and Relative Price Strength Percentile Three Months Ahead

$R2 = 0.9692$
Slope $= 0.3249$

– – BEST FIT PERCENTILES
—— ACTUAL PERCENTILES
········ Average Market Performance (50%)

Current Relative Price Strength Percentile, Rising Market

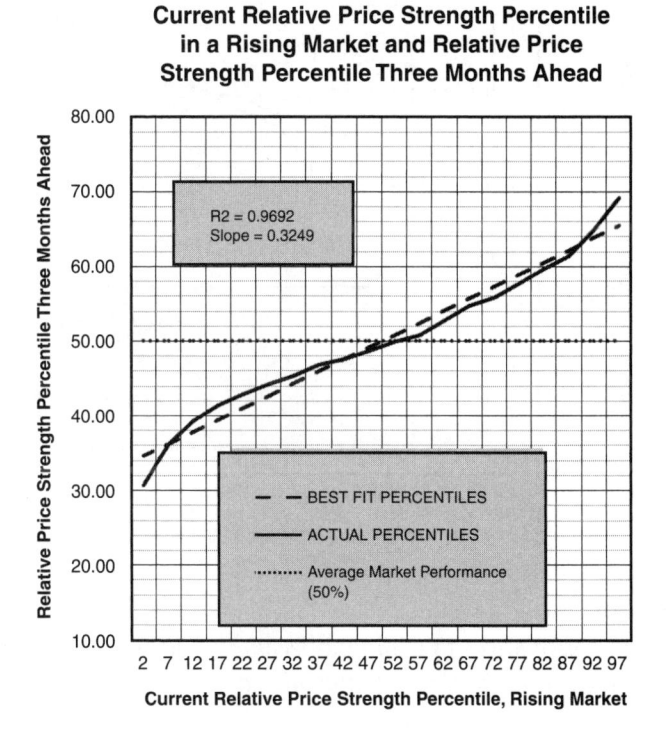

Figure 9.4
Current relative price strength in an advancing stock market versus relative price strength three months ahead

As in the three-month method for the entire market cycle, the best relative price strength rankings are those at the highest rankings. Selling can be held off until a stock's relative strength declines to the 52nd percentile or below if you can assure yourself that the market is bullish.

Current Relative Price Strength Percentile in a Declining Stock Market and Relative Price Strength Percentile Three Months Ahead

$R^2 = 0.9103$
Slope = 0.2928

- – – BEST FIT PERCENTILES
- —— ACTUAL PERCENTILES
- ······ Average Market Performance (50%)

Current Relative Price Strength Percentile, Declining Market

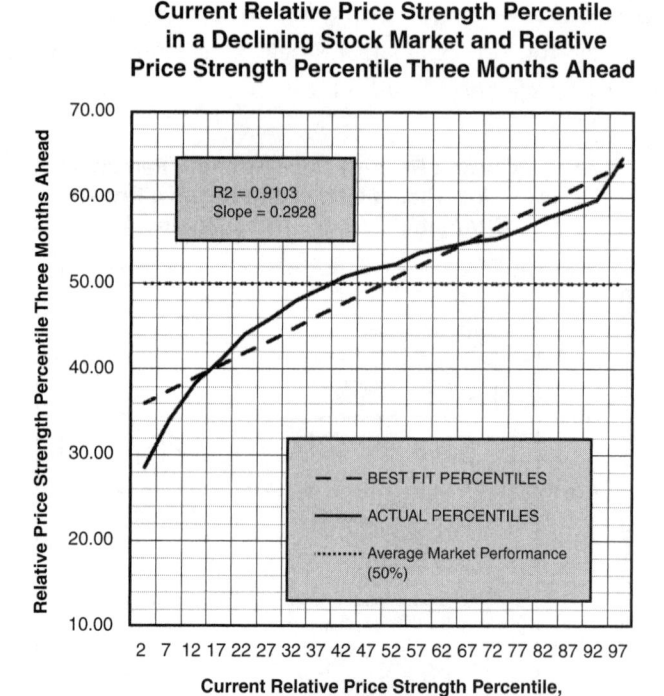

Figure 9.5
Current relative price strength in a declining stock market versus relative price strength three months ahead

Surprisingly, in a declining stock market, the use of relative price strength is equally as valid as in an advancing market as you can see in Figure 9.5. I would have assumed that in a declining stock market, the strongest stocks would be hit the hardest. This apparently is not true. The strongest stocks continue to be the strongest stocks over a three-month period ahead regardless of the market trend. In addition, the relative strength measure in a declining market has a stronger correlation to three-month performance than the relative price-to-sales by three and a half times and is infinitely better than relative reported earnings growth. This test again shows that relative price strength should be your primary selection criterion.

The best buying rank in a declining market is, as in other tests, the highest percentile in relative price strength, and the best selling rank is anything below the 37th percentile. Because the general market is declining, more stocks are also declining including stocks in the middle in relative strength. To avoid actual price loss, a higher level of percentile should be used as the selling rank in times of market decline. Use the bull market standard of the 52nd.

Summary

The best relative-price-strength-percentile buy and sell triggers for all markets, bull or bear, are shown in Table 9.1.

TABLE 9.1
Best Trigger Levels for Relative Price Strength Percentile Ranking

Trigger	Relative Ranking
Best Buy Zone	Highest possible rank
Best Sell Zone	Less than 52

Relative price strength, except for periods greater than six months, is a superior method of selecting stocks for future relative price performance. In order to get enough stocks to investigate in relative strength, I have used the top-ten percentiles. The 90+ level provides excellent performance over three months in both an advancing stock market and in a declining one. It also shows positive results over six months, though not as strongly, and even over 12 months, it has a slightly positive correlation. Any level less than the top 90th percentile and future performance gradually deteriorates. On the sell side, over three months, percentile 52 is the dividing level between positive and negative performance. Over six months, the dividing level declines to around the 37th percentile. In my past models, Growth and Value, I sold when stocks fell to the 30th percentile, but I am inclined to move the breakpoint up to the 52nd percentile.

Neither relative price strength nor relative reported earnings growth nor relative valuation has any predictive value 12 months in the future. For relative price strength, strong stocks are only temporarily strong and the efficient market hypothesis is correct in assuming that variations in price performance can occur, but eventually prices settle down to their value. One problem with this argument is that it assumes all investors invest for 12 months or more. Most other methods also fail to produce profits beyond 12 months. I liquidate a position only when one of its relatives changes to a sell level. At that point, I know the prospects are unfavorable for future performance over any period. To be successful with any method, you must constantly prune your portfolio to get rid of the stocks with little chance of profit and to add stocks as they meet your revised selection criteria. The concept of long-term investing or buy-and-hold has a flaw. This investment philosophy is not flexible enough to adjust to each stock's important characteristics and doesn't consider the more reliable correlations over shorter periods.

People always want an extra edge. I have been asked many times if looking at the change in relative strength rather than just the level would signal when specific stocks are preparing to rise. The answer is "no!" The change in relative price strength has no relationship to the subsequent price action of the stock. I have also been asked if I know what the underlying companies selected by relative price strength (or earnings growth or price-to-sales ratio) actually do for a business. In most cases, I don't know what the companies do. They are only symbols to me, and what they do only complicates the selection criteria and results. The numbers speak for themselves, and in all the screens in this book, no consideration was made for the business or peculiarities of specific companies or industries. I don't believe that looking at companies will help your portfolio performance. I know this attitude seems implausible and perhaps irresponsible, but I rely on the results of my tests. Extraneous information on specific companies had nothing to do with selecting stocks for the best subsequent performance.

CHAPTER 10

PUTTING IT TOGETHER

The most effective way to see whether a combination of any of the methods we have discussed can produce positive results over time is to test an imaginary portfolio in real time. This paper-trading approach can also be tested back in time, but such an experiment may suffer from "hindsight bias," whereby the tester is subtly influenced by knowing how the market performed during the test period. To avoid this bias, the imaginary portfolio should be created today and run into an unknown future. Unfortunately, this method takes time to complete and doesn't produce instant results. It is still the best method for testing a theory or system and is exactly how I tested the two imaginary portfolios, Growth and Value, over 25+ years.

Growth Model

In the summer of 1982, when I first began experimenting with relatives, I put together a hypothetical portfolio of stocks that were selected using relative earnings growth, relative price strength, and a chart pattern. I used the chart pattern for two reasons. First, I wanted to be sure that the relatively strong stock was actually rising, as this doesn't always happen in a steep market decline. Second, I wanted to provide a stop level that would automatically eject a stock from the portfolio if it declined by a predetermined amount. All these criteria were easily programmable and were left untouched for over 25 years. In other words, the computer did the selecting, the adding, and the deleting. This was an experiment, and I didn't have any real money invested with the system because, frankly, I didn't know if it would work. As it turned out, it worked well.

Definitions

A *stop order* is an order given to a broker to sell a stock at a specific price, the *stop price*, below its current price or to buy a stock at a specific price above its current price. When the stop price is reached, the order becomes a market order. The stop order is used as a protective order that gets you out of a position if it goes against you a certain price distance. For example, say a stock trades at $90, and believing it is a good stock and will rise, I buy it. I decide when I buy it that if the price declines to $80, I know I have made a mistake and must sell it. I place a sell stop order at $80 and limit my loss to $10.

In this manner, I have protected myself from major loss. This is called a *protective stop*. If I am right and the stock price advances, I move the stop upward, but always below the recent price. This is called a *trailing stop* and locks in my profit at a price above my original protective stop. I can also use an *entry stop* that is triggered when I want to buy a stock when it rises a certain amount or breaks above a certain level.

Stop Orders

In trading and investing, a sell stop order is an order placed with a broker to sell when a stock price falls to a specific price. Its purpose is to get rid of a stock that is not performing as expected as soon as possible, and thus, it is a valuable tool to minimize losses. Placements of sell stop orders can be tricky, however, because stocks fluctuate within their primary trend, and you don't want to get sold out on a fluctuation within a rising stock trend. The method I used was to determine the previous important support level, the previous low of importance at which the stock corrected and then reversed upward. If a stock rallies from one of these lows, buyers exist at that price level. If that level is penetrated, I know that the buyers are no longer there. If two of those levels are broken, I know I have a loser and must get rid of the stock.

Portfolio Construction

The imaginary portfolio was a list of stocks held in equal dollar amounts. This meant that I could just use the percentage changes of each stock rather than the value of each position to determine the list's performance. Using percentage changes assumes an equal dollar amount in each stock. Adjustments were made each week. An average of the percentage change of each stock in the portfolio was taken before any adjustments because it represented the performance of the list for the previous week. The percentage change of the portfolio each week was then compared to the S&P 500 and the Value Line Geometric, which is calculated in a similar manner. Transaction costs and dividends were not included, but likely offset each other. Figure 10.1 shows the cumulative performance of that portfolio as it appeared each week for over 25 years. At the end of the week, after the performance calculations, new stocks, if any, were added using the earlier criteria, and stocks that failed were eliminated from the list. This was the stock list for the following week called the Growth List.

Growth Model
July 1982 - December 1998

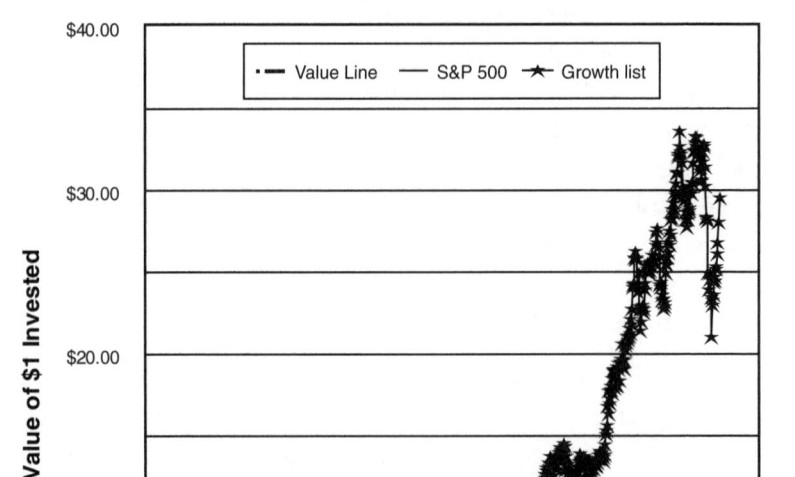

Figure 10.1
Weekly performance of a hypothetical growth portfolio using relative price strength, relative earnings growth, and chart pattern

The Growth List grew over the 25-year period by more than 100 times compared to only 13 times in the S&P and 6 times in the Value Line Geometric. This is an impressive performance. Some might criticize it because the turnover was close to twice a year and thus incurred many short-term capital gains, except in tax-free retirement accounts. This is a nonsensical argument, however, because if taxes took as much as 50 percent of the gains, the performance would still be four to five times higher than the S&P. Furthermore, it is almost impossible to forecast a long-term capital gain from existing information. The Growth List was run in real time and was published in my weekly letter. The list is still published today, and for the year ending December 2007 had better than tripled the S&P's percentage return.

Value Model

While growth was the first method to select stocks, I was also concerned about risk and how to prevent capital loss. One idea was to use something different than the chart pattern as a stop loss method. I created a new list called the "Value List" that was also tested live into the future to see whether its performance was as good or better than the "Growth List."

Change in Capital Risk Variables

In 1998, I realized that while the original list had performed well, I was worried because its performance had occurred primarily during the roaring bull market in the 1990s, one of the strongest in history. I was worried about what would happen if the market reversed direction, as it would eventually. My concern was not with the selection of additions to the list but with the capital risk. Would the system delete stocks in time to avoid capital loss, or should I find another approach to reduce capital risk? The standard method of technical analysis for reducing risk in individual positions is the use of stop orders. I found from past chart deletions that when a stock broke through the stop level, it had also declined enough in relative price strength to be eliminated through the relative strength sell trigger. The use of stops and the use of relative price strength were redundant. I had to come up with an additional or new method of reducing capital risk. During a declining market, a stock may have declined in absolute terms enough to be a serious risk to capital. The alternative to reducing risk through a sell discipline was to select only stocks that began with a lower than average risk, or stocks with low valuations. That would accomplish two things related to capital risk: It would keep the portfolio in value stocks where the beginning risk was low and it would not permit highly valued, overpriced stocks into the list. These latter are the most susceptible during a market decline.

When I read O'Shaughnessy's book *What Works on Wall Street*, I discovered from his tests that one way to potentially screen for risk initially was to use the price-to-sales ratio. Unlike O'Shaughnessy, who used the raw figure and set a limit, I used a relative calculation. I thought a set limit would not reflect changes in valuation as the market rose and declined and that a relative ratio would be more useful because it took out the influence of the market from the calculation. I calculated the relative price-to-sales ratio as outlined previously and arbitrarily selected only those stocks that had a relative price-to-sales ratio percentile of 30 or less. The relative price-to-sales ratio replaced the chart pattern stop as a means of reducing risk. I then created a new list and ran it every week from December 1998 to 2007. The performance of the list is shown in Figure 10.2.

Value Model

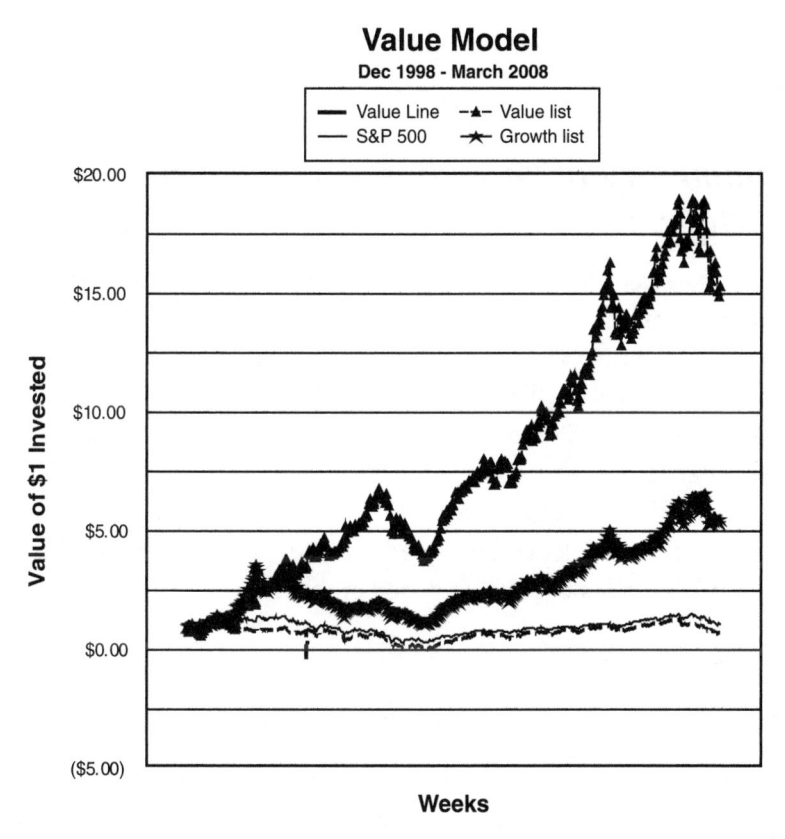

Dec 1998 - March 2008

[Chart showing weekly performance with Value Line, S&P 500, Value list, and Growth list; y-axis "Value of $1 Invested" from ($5.00) to $20.00; x-axis "Weeks"]

Figure 10.2
Weekly performance of a hypothetical portfolio using relative price strength, relative earnings growth, and relative price-to-sales ratio

The list (called the "Value List" because value was now introduced in the selection criteria in place of stop orders) outperformed both the averages and the original Growth List over the same tough period. It was a star. It had a rough correction during the 2000–2003 market declines, but it never became negative from the starting point at the top in 1998, as did the

S&P 500 and the Value Line Geometric during the broad market decline.

Summary of Growth and Value List Triggers

By selecting stocks, regardless of the background stock market, over a period as long as 25 years, the use of relatives, on a live basis without back testing, showed remarkable performance, beating the S&P 500 and the Value Line Geometric averages by wide margins. The holding period for stocks ran from an average of six months for the Growth List to over a year for the Value List. Each of the relative calculations is identical to the calculations used in the previous tests. The STRACT rules used are outlined in the following sections.

Growth List

To add a stock, it must meet the following conditions:

- Relative price strength greater than or equal to the 90th percentile (99 being the highest and zero being the lowest)
- Relative reported earnings growth greater than or equal to the 90th percentile
- Chart pattern showing an upward trend (two higher highs in a three-point reversal point-and-figure chart)
- Market capitalization of $1 billion or better
- Market price greater than or equal to $10

To delete a stock, it must meet only one of the following conditions:

- Relative price strength less than or equal to the 30th percentile
- Relative reported earnings growth less than the 70th percentile
- Chart break of two previous important lows

Value List

To add a stock, it must meet the following conditions:

- Relative price strength greater than or equal to the 90th percentile
- Relative reported earnings growth greater than or equal to the 90th percentile
- Relative price-to-sales ratio less than or equal to the 30th percentile
- Market capitalization of $500 million
- Market price greater than or equal to $10

To delete a stock, it must meet only one of the following conditions:

- Relative price strength less than or equal to the 30th percentile
- Relative reported earnings growth less than the 50th percentile
- Stocks are not deleted for extraordinarily high relative price-to-sales ratios

New Model (Called the "Bargain List")

As the result of these studies of relative selection methods, I decided to create a new list, called the "Bargain List" that would incorporate the best triggers found so far and would only include value and price strength. Several changes in the selection and deletion criteria were also included. I used the results of the tests of the relatives (see Chapters 7, "Value Selection," 8, "Relative Reported Earnings Growth Selection," and 9, "Relative Price Strength Selection") to create a new set of rules to select and delete stocks in an imaginary portfolio that will continue in the future. This hypothetical portfolio is calculated in the same manner as the Growth and Value Lists using equal stock investments each week for the two-year period from January, 2005 through December, 2007. The first year is from data already used in the tests, but the data since December of 2006 is new data that has not been incorporated in any tests.

Price-to-Sales

Better price performance was gained for both the three and six-month periods using relative price-to-sales ratio percentile rankings higher than the 17th percentile but not higher than around the 42nd percentile. From the evidence in my tests of the relative price-to-sales ratio, it became obvious that a relative valuation above the 42nd percentile or below the 7th percentile generally underperformed the market. *The Bargain List uses price-to-sales percentile levels from 17 to 42 for selecting stocks and uses the levels above 67 and below or equal to 7 for deleting stocks.*

Reported Earnings Growth

The best percentiles for three- and six-month performance in relative reported earnings growth were between the 42nd and the 87th. This is markedly different from the high percentiles I used in the earlier two lists and is kind of like saying the average stocks will perform with better results. Because the relative reported earnings percentiles demonstrated only a weak correlation and because their overall performance—especially in declining markets—was poor, *for the Bargain List I decided not to use the relative earnings growth technique as part of the model.*

Relative Price Strength

The correlation between relative price strength and latter performance is so strong and so smooth that it should be the primary method for selecting stocks in any model. Traditionally, I have selected the stocks above the 90th percentile. If not enough stocks are selected, and I want more, I just lower the required percentile in relative price strength to around the 80th percentile, but I don't change the thresholds for the other methods. They are not as important as relative price strength. As it turned out, the list of stocks using the 90th percentile was huge, much more than could be accommodated in a normal portfolio. *In the Bargain List, I selected stocks with a strength percentile equal to or above the 97th percentile.*

On the sell side, the percentile level when stocks begin to underperform out three to six months ranges between 37 and 52. I have always used the 30 level based on Levy's studies in the late 1960s but now change that sell trigger *for the Bargain List to any level equal to or below relative strength percentile 52.*

Bargain List Triggers

To add a stock, it must meet all the following conditions:

- Relative price strength percentile greater than or equal to 97
- Relative price-to-sales percentile greater than or equal to 17 and less than or equal to 42
- Market capitalization greater than or equal to $1 billion
- Market price greater than or equal to $10

In order to delete a stock, it must meet one of the following conditions:

- Relative price strength percentile less than or equal to 52
- Relative price-to-sales percentile less than or equal to 7 or greater than 67

Figure 10.3 shows the performance of the Bargain List as a hypothetical portfolio of stocks. The period over which the performance was measured was the two years from January 2005 through December 2007. However, Figure 10.3 shows only the performance for the year 2007. This performance is compared to the Value List that had been the best performing of the two earlier models in the period from January 1998 to December 2006. The data from 2006 had already been included in the earlier tests. This 2006 data is called "in-sample" data because its results are already included in the new Bargain List. A reliable system test must be run using "out-of-sample" data—data that has not been previously tested or used and is unknown to the model. The data for the year 2007 is this out-of-sample data. This is why only the 2007 performance results are shown. I ran the tests earlier on the data before 2007, created the Bargain

Model from that data, and then ran the Bargain List live through 2007 to see what would happen.

Bargain Model
January 2006 - March 2008

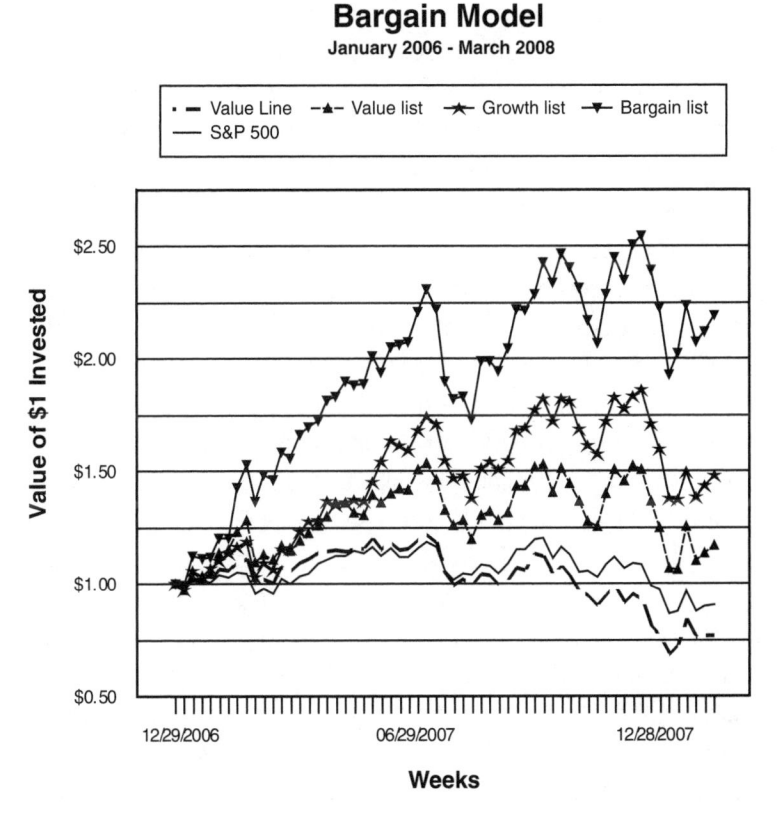

Figure 10.3
Performance of bargain list compiled from criteria derived from earlier tests of selection techniques compared to the best of the earlier models, the Value Model

During 2007, the Value List gained 25.3% and the Growth List gained 43.0%. The Bargain List gained 77.3%, more than 34 percentage points above either of the earlier lists. This is a sizeable and exciting difference for only one year's performance. Although the initial figures are terrific, the test should be run for several more years in both advancing and declining markets to see if its 2007 superior performance continues. I would not advise using this specific method yet, but we will know within a year whether it is reliable. The test shows that both lists likely outperformed even the best mutual funds and hedge funds. However, to remain safe from unknown effects, I would stick with the longer tested Value method for another year or two.

The creation and demonstration of the Bargain List is an example of how different techniques can be tested over time and with out-of-sample data. Some researchers take an earlier period and test their theory against a later period of time, all of which are known. For example, I could have taken the period from 1996 through 2000, an advancing period, along with 2000 through 2003, a declining period, to test the selection criteria, created a Bargain Model, and tested it against later data from 2003 through 2007. This method is most often used because it gives an instant result against data unknown to the model. Unfortunately, I have found that even though the out-of-sample in the tests is unknown to the model, it is known to the experimenter. The experimenter then is biased; knowing the ultimate market outcome can be an influence on how to create the model. The best, though most tedious method, is to create a model and then test it into the future where I, as the experimenter, have no possible knowledge of what will occur to the model's performance.

Summary

While the tests of the individual selection methods are interesting, the final proof must come from a practical application of

Putting It Together

these methods. To do this, I create hypothetical portfolios based on models using the best triggers (at the time of their inception) to see if in the future model can produce a better-than-market performance and thus justify the relative methods. In 1982 I began with the Growth List that has done well over the years and has remained consistent.

In 1998, I decided to change the risk selection from a chart stop to a relative valuation using the price-to-sales ratio. This was done at the time because I was fearful of a large market decline and was unsure as to what such an event would do to the Growth List. This new model was called the "Value List" and has been published weekly since then.

By 2006, the stock market had completed both a sizeable bull and bear run. I could now test the relative methods in both kinds of markets to see if the market background had any detrimental effects on performance. The results showed that relative reported earnings growth had little or no additional influence on future performance but that relative price-to-sales and relative price strength did. Relative price strength turned out to be the best selection method by far. A new hypothetical portfolio, the "Bargain List," was formed that is also running live every week at present. It has shown promise as an even more dynamic performer than the earlier models.

CHAPTER 11

SELECTING AND DELETING STOCKS

In Chapter 9, "Relative Price Strength Selection," and Chapter 10, "Putting It Together," I outlined the different uses of the relatives and gave trigger levels for buying and selling stocks. These boundaries are not written in stone. However, two aspects of investment should not be forgotten: buying and selling.

Buying

The buying decision is not necessary. You can remain with cash and not act. When you do decide to buy, you should have as much positive, tested information as possible. I emphasize the term "tested" because so many investors buy stocks without any idea of what they are doing. People invest on whims, bad information, and illogical reasoning. In some cases, I equate it with how the public bets on horses. One reason for this behavior is that tests of successful methods are few. Smart investors prefer to keep their methods to themselves or cannot describe them adequately. When tested, the methods that are used most often, such as earnings growth, price-to-earnings, and cash flow discount models, show mediocre results. Because these don't work that well, I see few studies of them. Therefore, those methods thought to be logical are rarely tested in public because their success rate is poor. Even professionals are unaware of how poorly these methods work. They were taught these methods in business school or by mentors or by professional associations, but they never questioned them because the methods seemed logical and everyone was using them.

Despite the declining market during the period, the buy trigger in ANR is still profitable as of March 21, 2008. This is not always the case, but Figure 11.1 shows an actual addition to the Bargain List when it occurred.

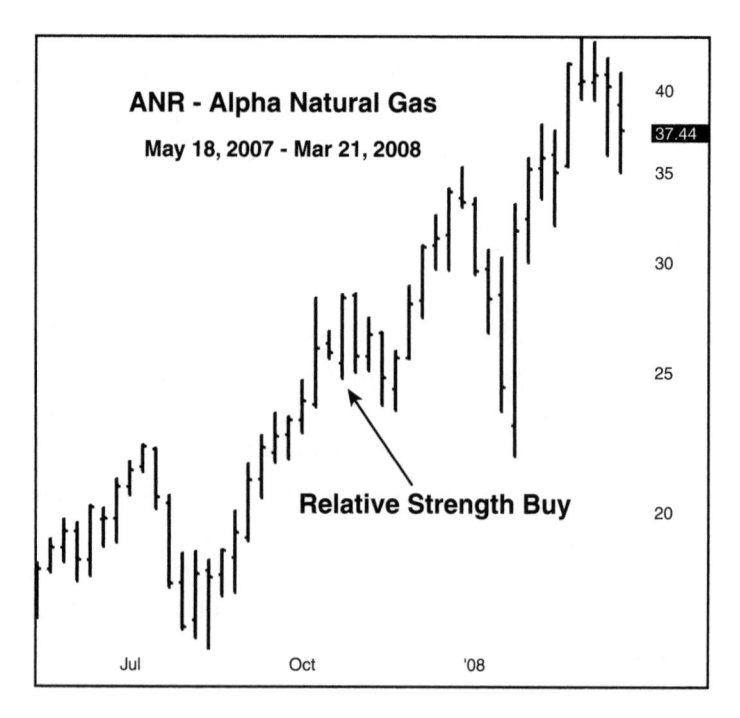

Figure 11.1
Alpha Natural Gas (ANR) for period May 18, 2007 to March 21, 2008, showing the point at which a buy trigger was signaled in the Bargain List

Selling

If you have bought a stock, you are going to have to sell it at some point. In many ways, the sell decision is not only the more difficult, but it is also the more important. It is difficult because you must act. Acting includes the risk that you might act incorrectly. The stock you sell might continue to rise. If you don't sell, the stock might decline. The best choice is to use tested and proven methods. The relatives provide excellent sell signals, and there is always the stop order to sell the stock at a predefined price, if you wish. You must use something to prevent loss, however. Untold millions of investors are severely hurt every year by not protecting their assets from price declines. I prefer the relative method because I have found it works better than a stop order. The various levels of relative price strength percentile used in the models are consistent and easy to apply. They remove a large element of the fear of making an incorrect decision and still reduce the risk of substantial loss.

The primary reason the sell decision is so important is that it determines your maximum risk. You always have a sell decision to make after you buy a stock. Using a sell discipline is the most logical and appropriate way to ensure that you know your capital risk going into the investment. I cannot emphasize enough how important a sell order is to maximizing your profits and limiting your losses. When you buy a stock, you immediately need to determine how the position should be sold, preferably when one of the sell techniques described earlier in the models is triggered. The STRACT setup is the holding of a specific position, the trigger is when one of the sell relative rankings is reached, and the action is to liquidate the position. You have seen the tests on what works best for selling. However, this is a difficult situation because you might want to keep the position, hoping that it will improve. "Hope" is not an investment method.

Remember how to define risk. It is not volatility, as the academics contend, but the exposure to the possibility of capital loss. You want to reduce the possibility of this exposure. Remember how the law of percentages works against you and that the more you lose capital, the more difficult it will be to regain it.

Risk of loss using the relatives is easy in an advancing market. For selling into a rising market, you will likely maintain a high portion of your profits if you use a high threshold, such as the 52nd percentile in relative price strength, unless the stock price plummets on some adverse news. If the market is declining, by definition, a stock trading with a 52nd percentile in relative price strength likely will be declining, and you will have already lost money on it. At this point, the sale is made to prevent further loss, and as long as the market is declining, further loss is highly probable. Some people are disturbed by the fact that selling with a loss will be necessary. They are the ones unable to accept that a small loss is better than a large one.

Other people are disturbed by having to wait until the stock reaches the 52nd percentile of relative price strength. They would prefer that the number be higher to avoid losses earlier. However, the statistics show that you will not avoid losses earlier and may even cause greater losses. The reason for these potential losses is that stocks do not always rise in a straight line. Instead, they tend to oscillate back and forth, sometimes correcting slightly and sometimes surging to new highs. On corrections, the relative price strength percentile often declines, sometimes as low as the 60 to 70 performance percentile rankings. If the stock is still stronger than all others, it will rebound upward, and the relative price rankings will rebound as well. But if the percentile for selling is too high, the possibility of selling the stock on just a minor downward oscillation is higher, and you may be out of a strong stock that is about to continue upward.

Selecting and Deleting Stocks

Like most things in life, it is a tradeoff between selling too early and missing an opportunity or avoiding a loss early and holding on longer and receiving a greater profit. The 52nd percentile ranking in relative price strength has been the best tradeoff between the two possible outcomes, at least in my experience and tests.

The deletion of Barnes Group in late November, 2007 eliminated it from the Bargain List. Figure 11.2 shows how relative strength can be used to prevent loss, sometimes substantial loss, regardless of the background market.

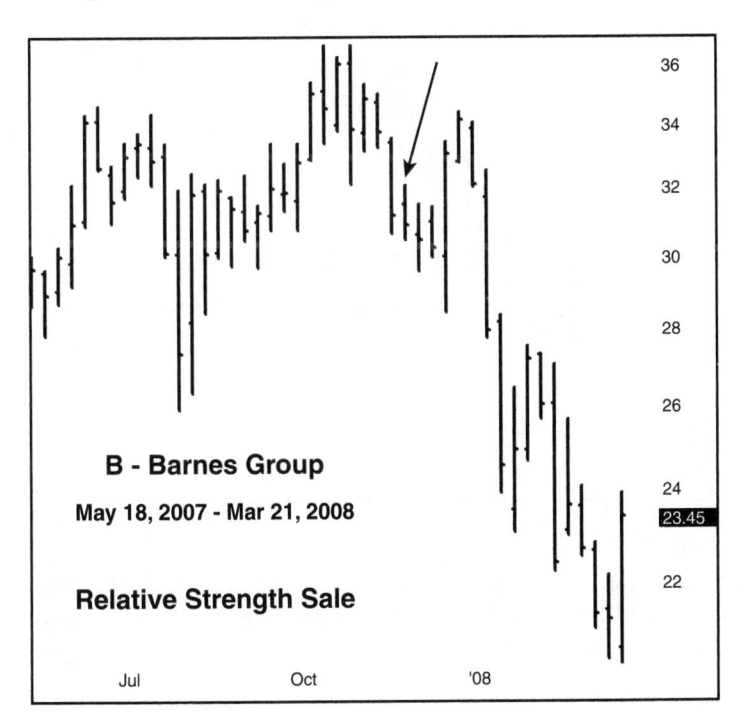

Figure 11.2
Barnes Group (B) May 18, 2007 to March 21, 2008, showing its deletion from the Bargain List on reaching a relative strength percentile of 52

Deletions from overly high valuations occur rarely. In Figure 11.3, CF Industries gave a sell trigger when it reached the 67th percentile ranking in price-to-sales. While such a trigger may not be the actual top of the price rise, it does signal when the risk of such a top has become likely.

Figure 11.3
CF Industries (CF) May 18, 2007 to March 21, 2008, showing the deletion from the Bargain List on reaching the 67th percentile in relative price-to-sales

Sources of Relative Information

To find those stocks that meet the right criteria, you need the correct percentile rankings.

You can calculate the rankings yourself. To do this, you need prices over at least 26 weeks, quarterly price-to-sales ratios, and earnings for the past five quarters. You must adjust this data each week for stock splits and other capital changes, symbol changes, and price errors. After you have cleaned the data, you must create programs to calculate the ratios and the rankings. Sources of raw price and fundamental data are relatively common if you wish to do the calculations yourself. They are listed in magazines such as *Technical Analysis of Stocks and Commodities* and *Futures Magazine*. This process is out of the question for most people, so looking for calculated data is the easiest way of finding the relatives.

I arranged with several firms that publish data to calculate the various rankings mentioned in this book. Others may come online in the future. The firms' websites are listed at www.charleskirkpatrick.com.

Finally, there is my own newsletter, the easiest way to proceed, that presents weekly the three models mentioned in this book, including the stocks in each, the additions and deletions, the rankings, the cost and present price, and a summary of each hypothetical portfolio's performance versus the market averages. The newsletter is also available through www.charleskirkpatrick.com.

Other Concerns

Let's get rid of some potential concerns. The first is always the cost of execution, including commissions and the costs of transacting buy and sell orders. Commissions should be of little concern provided you use a discount broker. The lowest charges I have seen recently for regular investors are around 50 cents per 100 shares of stock. Brokers have different scales based on the sizes of orders and the frequency of trading. There is usually a minimum charge, especially on orders of less than 100 shares. These fees are constantly changing and require that you keep up with the latest charges. In any case, 50 cents on 100 shares is so low as to be irrelevant to your performance.

Costs for gathering the information to calculate the various percentiles can be as inexpensive as subscribing to a service that already does the calculations to writing the programs and gathering market data yourself, or even using free research services provided by many online discount brokerages. Even if you do subscribe to a fee-based service, it should run less than a few hundred dollars a year unless you contemplate performing a sophisticated analysis.

How to Act

Of course, if you decide there is merit to the methods mentioned here, you can assemble the stocks for a hypothetical and actual portfolio with just the data on rankings. You may prefer to adjust the models to include or not include any of the methods and you may adjust the parameters for buying and selling. This would be the advantage of using one of the providers of the rankings mentioned previously. Or, you may prefer to follow the models precisely. Regardless of your choice of action, in Appendix A, "Investment Procedure Example," I outline the step-by-step procedure for using outside services to create a portfolio based on the Value Model and using a moving average portfolio capital risk method to reduce losses in case of a large market decline. If you wish to change the procedure, you can use Appendix A as a guide.

CREATING AND MANAGING A PORTFOLIO

Appendix A shows how you can do most of the work yourself using other sources of data. The easiest is to have the calculations already done for you.

Using the Kirkpatrick Market Strategist (KMS), you will have all the necessary calculations each week. All you need to do is spend an hour at most to realign your portfolio based on the changes shown in the letter and then place the required orders with your broker.

The KMS is a market newsletter that is emailed once a week over the weekend. Aside from some short commentary on the stock and bond markets, it includes all the information you need to manage your own stock investments using the methods outlined in this book. It lists the stocks currently in the Value Growth, and Bargain Lists, when they were added to the list, any new additions or deletions for each week, profit or loss in each stock, and how much percentage cash should be held in reserve for a declining stock market.

Let's walk through a recent period so as to show how KMS could have been used. We will assume the use of the Value List as our model will add and delete stocks as they fulfill the criteria for the list and adjust for any reserve cash positions as we go along. We will assume the equal dollar value approach and the moving average risk method to determine exactly how much stock to buy or sell.

On July 27, 2007 through August 24, 2007, we will begin with $100,000. It could be any amount but this is an easy number to use. On July 27, 2007, KMS states that the Value portfolio should be invested 75 percent in stocks. This means that of your $100,000, only $75,000 will be invested in equal proportions in the Value List. That list included AAR Corp, AK Holding,

Anixter, CIGNA Corp, Crown Holdings, Cubic Corp, Encore Wireless, General Cable, Geo Group, Kaman Corp, Sun Healthcare, Terex Corp, United Rentals, U.S. Steel, Valero Energy, and Warnaco. This is 16 stocks. Dividing your $75,000 by 16 gives you around $4,700 per stock. Dividing the price per share of each stock into $4,700 gives you the number of shares to purchase. You are now 75 percent invested in the Value List.

On August 3, 2007, the following week, the percentage to be invested is reported in KMS as 50 percent. In addition, U.S. Steel is deleted from the list. This means you must sell all your U.S. Steel, and cut back on all the other positions until you have the remaining stocks in equal dollar amounts equal to 50 percent of your portfolio market value. Total stocks are now 15.

On August 10, 2007, two stocks are added to the Value List: Fresh Del Monte and Owens Illinois, and two stocks are deleted: AK Holding and Encore Wireless. You must now balance your holdings by taking the total number of stocks (15) and dividing it into 50 percent of your total market value, including cash. This will give you the dollar amounts of each of the 15 stocks you should hold. You enter buy and sell orders to adjust each stock position in line with the calculations just done and still have 50 percent of your assets in cash.

On August 17, 2007, General Cable is deleted from the list and is sold from your portfolio. Because there are no stock additions, you must realign all your positions to equal dollar amounts that add up to 50 percent of your portfolio total value.

On August 24, 2007, KMS reports that the percentage invested in the Value List should be raised to 75 percent of total portfolio value. You adjust each position to account for this change. You are now 75 percent invested.

All the steps necessary are mentioned in this example. The time to figure adjustments and enter orders with your broker should be minimal. Your results should then closely follow the hypothetical Value portfolio mentioned each week in KMS. It's as easy as that.

Summary

As opposed to just experimenting with the relative methods, the true test comes from creating a practical portfolio that outperforms the market averages. To do this, specific buys and sells must be made with the discipline suggested by the test results. The buy decision is relatively easy because it can be avoided. The sell decision, however, cannot be avoided. Fortunately, the relative method provides specific triggers for selling as well as buying. They should be used.

The actual transaction costs of buying and selling today are ridiculously low and irrelevant to performance. There should be no hesitancy to act once a reliable trigger presents itself.

The portfolio management process requires not only the selection and deletion of stocks but money management as well. Where reliable sell triggers reduce the risk of capital loss in individual stocks, money management reduces the risk of capital loss from the entire market. Several methods of money management are presented in the next chapter.

CHAPTER 12

CREATING A PORTFOLIO OF STOCKS

One method of preventing major loss is to avoid the market entirely when it is declining. This brings in another testing problem, that of timing the market rather than just individual stocks. Timing the market, using the reaction theory versus the prediction theory, is best done through creating a portfolio that includes specific rules.

You may now realize that you should never try to predict anything connected with the markets. You know the stock market is the best investment vehicle over time, but it often has serious corrections that you would like to avoid. You now know what techniques are important in the selection and deletion of stocks, and you know how to use them. You may protect yourself from capital risk in individual stocks, but you also have to protect yourself from losing your capital in a large market decline. You need to learn how to integrate this knowledge to reduce capital risk.

Maximum Drawdown

To determine the risk of capital loss, the maximum drawdown in the Value and Growth Lists, the S&P 500, and the Value Line Geometric was calculated. Table 12.1 shows that the percentage of maximum drawdowns during the four large market corrections since 1982 were substantial. The Growth List, the only one to have existed through the entire period, had a larger drawdown than both the S&P 500 and the Value Line Geometric, despite its superior overall performance.

TABLE 12.1
Maximum Drawdowns During Market Corrections from 1982–2007

Market Corrections	Growth List	Value List	S&P 500	Value Line Geometric
1987	–42.3%		–31.2%	–34.5%
1989–1990	–26.9%		–16.5%	–35.0%
1998	–36.7%		–14.3%	–31.3%
2000–2002	–54.1%	–37.4%	–46.9%	–46.7%

These statistics show that the danger of market decline is considerable. Even with excellent stock selection alone, capital risk is large. The S&P 500 declined almost 50 percent in the bear market between 2000 and 2002. There are no havens in such a market. A method to reduce this risk requires portfolio management.

Simple but Practical Methods of Creating a Portfolio

A portfolio must be simple to manage, inexpensive to operate, profitable, and reduce the risk of capital loss. Capital loss can come from individual stocks as well as the entire portfolio reacting to a general market decline. Just because it may hold the strongest and best stocks, it still can suffer through a declining market.

Three Methods of Creating a Portfolio

Serious declines occur over long periods, as do advances. You have the choice of either keeping the stocks, adjusting them as the model you select suggests, or using a market timing method to reduce your investment exposure during a market decline.

Keeping Fully Invested

You can ride your portfolio up and down with the market just as my three model tests have done. The performance figures in Figures 10.1 and 10.2 show how successful these methods have been without adjusting for the market risk. Just like the models, you keep the balance of stocks in your portfolio in equal portions from week to week. As stocks are deleted and cash is raised, the money you earn is used either to purchase new stocks that have been selected or is spread among the existing stocks. If no stock is deleted and a new one is added, you must sell enough of each existing position to have all the stocks, new and existing, equally represented. This method requires constant adjusting of stock holdings to keep everything even, but it has shown excellent performance. The switches need not be done every week, and as one stock begins to outperform the pack, it need not be sold right away, but periodically, monthly at least, the portfolio should be adjusted so that each stock in the model list is equally proportioned in your portfolio.

There are problems with this, however. I dislike the method of creating this kind of portfolio because it is time-consuming and expensive. It also violates the rule of relative price strength because if a stock is particularly strong one week, a small portion of it is sold the next week to bring it into line. This means you are selling a portion of the strongest stocks and likely buying more of the weaker stocks. It is the most conservative way of watching the performance of a list of stocks, but it is not the most practical for use in the real world.

Another problem with this method is that the portfolio is invested 100 percent of the time and is unable to adjust to any major market decline. As stocks are deleted, the amount invested in the remaining stocks increases to maintain the equality of each position. This means that capital risk may become substantial. The hypothetical lists used in the last chapter were always 100 percent invested because I did not want a market direction component in the results. I was looking at what would happen only when certain selection and deletion requirements were met. As a result, during the weak stock market in 2000–2002, the lists suffered along with the market (see Table 12.1). They recovered quickly because the selection methodology was accurate, but they still suffered a large decline when the market suffered. Had they had some method of adjusting the portfolio as the market became weak, it would have kept the portfolio from losing that significant amount during the decline. Soon after the market bottom, the portfolio with some means of raising cash to protect assets would be in a better position to take advantage of the lower price. Some critics maintain that it would have been better to hold the list throughout the declining period, but they would not know at the time the market began to decline just how far it would go.

Thus, the cash pulled from the market was worth the risk of losing assets, and it certainly was more calming to the investor's nerves than watching the portfolio being destroyed during tough times. After all, it took roughly 25 years for the market after the 1929 crash to recover to where it had been. That is a long time to wait to get even on your investments.

Adjusting for Market Capital Risk Using a Maximum Number of Stocks

There are two ways to reduce market capital risk in a portfolio. The first is to assume you will be invested at the maximum in a fixed number of stocks, say 20, for example. You divide the total amount you are investing, say $50,000, by the maximum number of stocks you wish to own to determine how much you will invest in each stock. In this example, a $2,500 investment in each stock of 20 stocks, regardless of how many are on the model list, would be the standard position. Stocks are then bought or sold as they are selected or deleted from the model list. This gives the portfolio an automatic adjustment to market conditions. For example, if you decide that you want a maximum of only 20 stocks in your portfolio, and your combined method of adding and deleting stocks can come up with only ten stocks that meet your criteria, you will automatically be 50 percent invested. You will own 10 of your potential 20 stocks. The remaining cash would be invested in a stable, safe fixed-income issue such as the U.S. Treasury Bill, often called a "cash equivalent" because it can be turned in for cash with almost no wait. All investment positions can be kept in their original amount, taking advantage of the particularly strong ones and reducing the amount of adjusting. When the selection criteria suggest that a specific stock should be sold, the proceeds are added to the portfolio and a new dollar amount is calculated for the next investment based on the 1/20 of the entire investment portfolio of stocks and cash equivalents. No new stock is purchased until it appears as an addition on the model used. In short, you invest only in those stocks that are selected by the model up to the maximum limit you establish. When a sale takes place from the model deleting a stock, you keep the proceeds in cash unless there is a new stock suggested or there exists a stock on the model list that you don't own that still meets the criteria for selection by the model.

When you have a portfolio of stocks less than the maximum number you established, the low number of attractive stocks indicates that the market is weak and your portfolio is automatically adjusting to that weakness by selling stocks and not buying more. You don't have to make any predictions of future markets; you just react to what the market offers.

This method also can include leverage in a bull market. Should the market be particularly strong and say 30 stocks meet the selection criteria, the $50,000 portfolio would be 150 percent invested (30 x $2,500 = $75,000). This would require borrowing on margin $25,000 or changing the rule for maximum number of issues you wish to hold. Of course, the borrowing of money to invest is especially dangerous and not suggested. Remember that borrowed money buried the hedge funds. Instead, you can just ignore stocks added to the list when the number exceeds your maximum and you are invested fully to the maximum. Add new stocks only at that point when a stock is sold.

The maximum amount of stocks is purely up to you. It is based on the maximum number of stocks selected during a rising market under normal conditions as well as on the amount of capital available. If your selection method suggests that 50 stocks meet the criteria, you should tighten the criteria so that fewer stocks are selected. A portfolio of 50 stocks becomes unwieldy. The usual amount is around 20. Another method of reducing the amount of stocks to consider in an especially long list is to take every other stock, thus cutting your list in half, and creating an imaginary model list from just these stocks. In the example of 50 stocks on a list, you would then have only 25 to be concerned with.

This portfolio type can also use the moving average crossovers described next as an additional protection against market decline.

Adjusting for Market Capital Risk Using Simple Moving Averages

Another method is less complex but also less reliable because it waits for your portfolio to actually decline in value before kicking in. This is the use of simple moving averages of your hypothetical portfolio or model market value (your actual portfolio may be differing from the model depending on your method of buying and selling. It is important that you use the model value not your portfolio value). My standard is 12 weeks, 26 weeks, and 52 weeks. Every week, I compare the current model value to the 12-, 26-, and 52-week simple moving averages. If the current model value declines below its 12-week moving average, I sell 25 percent of my portfolio. If the current model value declines below its 26-week moving average, I sell down to a total 50 percent invested in stocks, leaving me with 50 percent in cash equivalents. I am now gradually raising cash based on the poor performance of the model value. Should the model value decline below its 52-week moving average, I sell everything. Such a dire occurrence suggests that the stock market is in a long-term decline. I will suffer losses initially, but my chances of being wiped out are eliminated. This way, I can never be ruined by a major decline and will have cash when the market direction reverses upward.

The process is reversed after a major decline that has forced me to raise 100 percent cash or any other cash level. When the current model value rises above its 12-week simple moving average, I buy enough stock to account for 25 percent of my total intended investment. As the various crossovers occur, my cash is adjusted accordingly—another 25 percent for a rise above its 26-week moving average and fully invested above all its moving averages. In an advance from a major bottom, I will likely have to wait for positive crossovers, but the risk of holding cash eliminates any worry about losing capital.

You can use any period for the moving averages and any combination of signals. Just be careful that the period of the moving average is relatively long. Otherwise, you will be buying and selling frequently with little to show for your efforts. Figure 12.1 demonstrates the results of the Value List being adjusted periodically for my standard 12-, 26- and 52-week moving average system.

The use of the moving average technique on the Value Model shows several periods of market weakness that were avoided. The most prominent is the period from the middle of 2002 through early 2003 when the Value Model was declining sharply. Notice the flat phase in the adjusted line during that period. This is when the model was 100% in cash and not exposed to the market decline. This occurred again when the model turned weak in late 2004 and early January 2008. The problem with using such a method is that it is usually late in recovering from the decline because it needs the moving averages to turn upward. Often a market coming out of a major bottom will rise rapidly before the moving averages can catch up. Thus, the overall performance of the adjusted model is less than the actual model, but the risk of a major loss is also reduced. You will also note, however, that the adjusted model still outperformed the S&P 500 by a substantial margin. This is the method used in the KMS newsletter for hypothetical portfolios and its usage is shown in Chapter 11, "Selecting and Deleting Stocks."

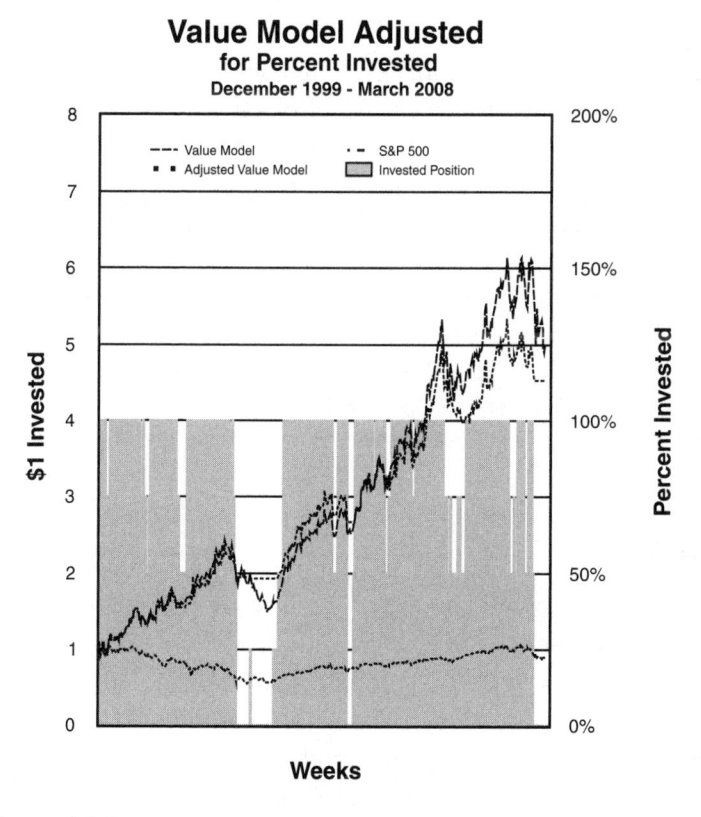

Figure 12.1
Effect of moving average signals

Maximum Drawdowns

Table 12.2 shows that for every correction since 2001, the moving average method has either registered the same maximum drawdown or something considerably less. This demonstrates the usefulness of the moving average method in reducing capital loss, especially in a major correction such as those that occurred 2002–2003 and in 2007–2008.

TABLE 12.2
Maximum Drawdowns for Market Corrections Using Fully Invested and Moving Average Method in the Value List

Dates of Correction	Using Fully Invested Model	Using Moving Average Adjustments to Reduce Market Risks
May 18, 2001–June 22, 2001	–12.8%	–12.4%
May 24, 2002–March 21, 2003	–38.5%	–16.7%
July 16, 2004–August 6, 2004	–11.6%	–11.6%
May 5, 2006–September 22, 2006	–18.4%	–19.9%
October 12, 2007–March 7, 2008	–18.4%	–11.3%

Summary

In this chapter, I suggest only a few ways to organize your portfolio. These are the simplest and require the least amount of calculating. It is possible to become much more complicated and introduce hedging concepts and so forth, but I don't believe they improve performance over the methods demonstrated. Usually the simplest is the easiest to understand and to manage.

The basics for any portfolio, aside from keeping it simple, are to profit and reduce the risk of losing capital. What is important is that you do not lose large amounts of money. It takes a long time to make it back no matter how good your investment model may be.

So, now you won't have to listen to the news or worry about your positions because the portfolio will adjust by itself. The selling criteria will warn you when to delete a stock, the buy criteria will give you a list of new selections, and your portfolio construction will keep you relatively safe from a market disaster. You won't sell at the top or buy at the bottom, but you hopefully will receive an outstanding return with minimal capital risk in case the market goes awry. In other words, for a little bit of work on a consistent basis, you will beat the big guys and not get clobbered like they do in a major decline.

Conclusion

I have shown you how the use of relatives has worked for the past 20+ years. While I can never be sure that it will work in the future, the past is certainly a positive guide. Can the techniques in this book fail in the future? Of course they can, just as any investment method can fail. I am hoping, however, that the past success of these techniques is related to human nature, emotion, and bias rather than to logic. Logic or rational thinking often fails because all the possible variables are not necessarily known or considered. However, if the success of the relatives is due to how our brains have been collectively wired throughout our creation, it is unlikely that it will change until some exogenous event causes a mutation in humans that favorably affects rationality. We like to think we are rational, just as we like to think we can control the climate and are the center of the universe, but we aren't and thank goodness. If we didn't have our herd instincts or our aversion to loss or many other biases, the markets might act rationally, and we would then be unable to profit. As long as the human race can become excited or morose, affected by greed and fear, stocks will travel under and above their true value, travel in trends, and make the relatives useful. Good luck!

APPENDIX

INVESTMENT PROCEDURE EXAMPLE

In this exercise, I systematically walk you through the procedures for investing with the methods used in this book. I assume that I am investing in the Value Model with a moving average signal for portfolio protection.

Finding Data, Calculating Data, and Locating Sources

Other ranking services can be found through the data services mentioned in my website—www.charleskirkpatrick.com. I vetted these services and found them to be accurate and timely. One advantage of the data services is that you can check on other stocks that you own to see how they stack up against the ideal. You can also change the levels for adding and deleting stocks from your hypothetical portfolio as you choose by changing what you consider better percentile levels. The data services, therefore, provide you with more flexibility to do analysis by yourself.

The Hypothetical Value Model Portfolio

Under all circumstances, you should create a list of the stocks in your portfolio, their values, and whatever cash equivalents you hold. This is necessary no matter what portfolio structure you decide to use. Usually your broker provides a portfolio valuation (at least daily), but if he doesn't, you should prepare one at least weekly. It is from this report that you adjust your positions based on the stocks added or deleted from the Model list, which is based on the model you select for portfolio structure.

If you wish to use the moving average method for reducing portfolio capital risk, you must create a hypothetical portfolio with the criteria you decide to use in practice and your actual portfolio report. This provides you with a measure of the success or failure of your method and is necessary to calculate the moving average values of your hypothetical portfolio. It should include the name of each stock in the portfolio and the price by date each week it is held. From this table, you can calculate the performance of the list that assumes an equal invested position in each stock. An example of a spreadsheet is shown in Table A.1.

The first column lists the name of the stock. This is followed by two columns per week; the first is the stock's price for that week and the second is the percentage change of the stock for that week calculated as a ratio of the current price to the previous week's price. A stock that rises from 10 to 12 would have a ratio of 1.20. A stock that declines from 10 to 9 would have a ratio of 0.90. This is done to minimize the effect of percentage changes on performance. If a stock price is zero, it was deleted from the list the previous week and is no longer followed. Along the top of the table is a date for each week and an average of all the performance ratios. This latter figure tells you the average

Investment Procedure Example

Table A.1
Hypothetical Value Portfolio for December 28, 2007 through January 18, 2008

STOCK	12/28 PRICE	01/04 PRICE	RATIO	01/11 PRICE	RATIO	01/18 PRICE	RATIO
Higher performance			1.0451		1.0690		1.0008
Low performance			0.8236		0.8672		0.8000
Average of all stocks			0.9442		0.9515		0.9190
AAR Corp	37.78	35.18	0.9312	30.70	0.8727	27.23	0.8870
AGCO Corp	68.71	68.14	0.9917	63.80	0.9363	57.81	0.9061
AK Steel	45.52	41.43	0.9101	37.57	0.9068	37.18	0.9896
Bunge Corp	119.03	121.00	1.0166	129.35	1.0690	109.12	0.8436
CNH Global NV	66.55	66.07	0.9928	58.80	0.8900	55.54	0.9446
Cubic Corp	39.95	34.28	0.8581	31.36	0.9148	0.00	sold
Foster L. B.	51.63	47.82	0.9262	42.16	0.8816	39.93	0.9471
Humana Inc	76.04	79.47	1.0451	84.28	1.0605	84.35	1.0008
Interface Inc.	16.42	15.10	0.9196	0.00	sold		
Kaman Corp	36.49	37.73	1.0340	32.72	0.8672	29.47	0.9007
Owens Illinois	50	45.58	0.9116	45.71	1.0029	41.37	0.9051
UAP Holding	38.59	38.81	1.0057	38.75	0.9985	38.13	0.9840
W R Grace	26.13	21.52	0.8236	21.90	1.0177	17.52	0.8000
Warnaco	34.50	29.40	0.8522	0.00	sold		

performance of the hypothetical portfolio for the week, and it is used to calculate your hypothetical portfolio performance over time and to calculate moving averages. Your own portfolio should do as well, or close. The two rows at the top show the highest and lowest individual stock performances for that week. This information is useful to screen for stock splits and other errors that might creep into the calculations.

Performance of Value Model

If you are interested in following the performance of your hypothetical portfolio to calculate the moving-average, portfolio-protection method, Table A.2 shows the necessary calculations. The moving average calculation must be done on the hypothetical portfolio and not a market average or your own portfolio. The hypothetical portfolio may perform quite differently than a market average, and you don't want to be limited by the market average performance. In Figure 12.1, for example, you can see that the Value List continued to rise even when the S&P 500 was beginning its decline. The Value List continued to rise into early 2002, whereas the S&P 500 had been declining since the middle of 2000. The model should be invested in the strongest stocks, those that keep performing long after the general market has begun to decline. The calculations that use the moving average system should be based only on the model, not the market averages nor your portfolio value.

Table A.2
Performance Spreadsheet for Value Model

Date	ValMod	Chg	S&P	VLG
08/03/2007	5.838	0.9705	1433.06	456.92
08/10/2007	5.893	1.0095	1453.64	463.71
08/17/2007	5.684	0.9645	1445.94	457.10
08/24/2007	5.959	1.0483	1479.37	468.57
08/31/2007	6.005	1.0077	1473.99	466.79
09/07/2007	5.901	0.9828	1453.55	458.35
09/14/2007	5.989	1.0149	1484.25	462.51
09/21/2007	6.292	1.0505	1525.75	474.78
09/28/2007	6.293	1.0002	1526.75	472.87

Table A.2 shows a number of columns in the middle of 2007. The left column is the date for the week. The next column to the right is the hypothetical value of the Value List as of that date (carried forward from the year 2000). The next column is the percentage change for the week taken from the calculations in Table A.1. This percentage change is multiplied by the previous week's model value (column to the left) to arrive at a new value for the current week. To the right of the model percentage change is the S&P 500 and to its right is the Value Line Geometric Average. You can compare the performance of each by measuring the percentage change over any dates. For example, the percentage change in the model from August 3 to September 28 is +7.70 percent (6.293/5.838−1) versus +6.53 percent for the S&P 500 (1526.75/1433.06−1).

You don't need to go through all the calculations if you are not using the moving average method of reducing portfolio risk.

Adding and Deleting Stocks

Your next problem is what to do with additions and deletions as they appear based on the model you choose. For example, the Value List deletes stocks when they decline below the 30th relative strength percentile or decline below the 50th relative reported earnings growth percentile. These are the only criteria for a stock to be deleted from your portfolio if you follow the Value List, and no stock should be deleted until it has reached at least one of the deletion criteria. The model, therefore, makes the decision for you as to when and what to sell. This way, you don't know when you will sell, but you do know that you will hold the stock position as long as its odds are favorable. After the odds turn against the position, you must sell it immediately. Not all stocks will be deleted at a profit, of course, because you want to guard against capital loss in those stocks that become weak. In other words, you profit by holding the strong stocks and selling the weak stocks.

TRICKS FOR BUYING AND SELLING

A trick to adding or deleting to or from your portfolio is to use stop orders. This method is also applicable when you first start and want to know which stocks to purchase from an existing list. If buying, take the previous week's high price and enter a buy stop order just above it. If the stop is triggered, you know you have a strong stock. If it is not triggered, the stock is weaker than before and you have no position in it until it becomes strong again. If nothing is triggered, continue to adjust the buy stop price each following week to slightly above the previous week's high price until it is triggered or the stock is deleted from the list. The same process in reverse with sell stops can be used for stocks deleted from the list. Simply enter a sell stop order

Investment Procedure Example

slightly below the previous week's low. Often, when a stock is deleted from a list, it rebounds for a week or two. Using this method, you may pick up a few extra points.

The buy decision depends on the portfolio type you want to use. If you use the geometric system, you are fully invested at all times. You must rearrange the holdings in your portfolio into even dollar amounts. This requires occasional buying and selling small portions to align the stock positions equally, and when a new stock is added, you must sell portions of held stock to raise the cash needed to buy the new stock. When a stock is sold and not replaced, you must then use the cash received to apportion the positions equally in the other stocks, always remaining fully invested. This method should consider the moving average method of protecting against market risk.

If you decide to use the limited holding portfolio where you restrict the portfolio to a maximum number of stocks, adding a stock as it is selected is relatively easy. You know the value of your portfolio and you know the number of stocks you want to hold at a maximum. Just divide the maximum holding number into the total portfolio value, and you then know the maximum amount of cash to place in each position, even if there are only a few stocks showing up as favorable in your model. Using Table A.1, for example, and assuming a maximum holding of 20 stocks allowed, only 11 stocks are on the list. Thus, you would buy 11 positions and keep the remaining cash for future purchases should they arise. In the meantime, your portfolio is invested only slightly more than 50 percent, and your exposure to a major market decline is reduced.

There are, of course, many models to choose for stock selection and deletion criteria and for portfolio systems to arrange your stocks and protect against market risk. It is up to you to decide which series of models and methods to use.

REFERENCES

Brooks, Robert E. and J. Brian Gray. "History of the Forecasters: An Assessment of the Semi-Annual U.S. Treasury Bond Yield Forecast Survey as Reported in the *Wall Street Journal*." University of Alabama finance working paper No. 03-06-01, 2003.

Burnham, Terry. *Mean Markets and Lizard Brains: How to Profit from the New Science of Irrationality*. New York: John Wiley & Sons, Inc., 2005.

Dreman, David and Michael A. Berry. "Analyst Forecasting Errors and Their Implications for Security Analysts." *Financial Analysts Journal*. May–June, 1995.

Elgers, Peiter T., May H. Lo, and Ray J. Pfeiffer, "Delayed Security Price Adjustments to Financial Analysts' Forecasts of Annual Earnings," *Accounting Review*, Vol. 76, No 4, October, 2001: pp. 613–632.

Federal Reserve Bank of Boston Economic Quiz, www.bos.frb.org/economic/quiz/q102102.cfm (study on results of *Wall Street Journal* survey).

Francis, Jennifer and Donna R. Philbrick. "Analysts' Decisions as Products of a Multi-Task Environment." *Journal of Accounting Research*, 31: 2, Autumn, 1994: 216–230.

Jegadeesh, Narasimhan and Sheridan Titman. "Returns to Buying Winners and Selling Losers: Implications for Stock Market Efficiency." *Journal of Finance*, 1993: 43, 65–91.

_____ . "Profitability of Momentum Strategies: An Evaluation of Alternative Explanations." *Journal of Finance*, 2001: 56, 699–720.

Kirkpatrick, Charles D., Market Strategist, www.charleskirkpatrick.com.

Levy, Robert A. "Relative Strength as a Criterion for Investment Selection." *Journal of Finance*, 1967: 22:4, 595–610.

_____. Predictive Significance of Five-Point Chart Patterns." *Journal of Business*. Chicago, IL: University of Chicago, 1971.

Lo, Andrew W. *A Non-Random Walk Down Wall Street*, Princeton, NJ: Princeton University Press, 1999.

Lo, Andrew W. and A. Craig MacKinlay. "Stock Market Prices Do Not Follow Random Walks: Evidence from a Simple Specification Test." *Review of Financial Studies*, 1988: 1, 41–66.

Mandel, Michael. "Bad Forecasts." *BusinessWeek*, January 3, 2006.

Merrill, Arthur A. *Filtered Waves*. Self-published privately by the author, 1997.

Motley Fool. Mutual Fund Center: Mutual Funds: Performance, www.fool.com/school/mutualfunds/performance/record.htm (comments by John Bogle on mutual fund performance).

O'Shaughnessy, James P. *What Works on Wall Street*. New York: McGraw-Hill, 1997.

Ritholtz, Barry. "Apprenticed Investor: The Folly of Forecasting." *Real Money.com*, June 7, 2005.

Sagi & Seasholds. "Firm Specification Attributes and Cross-Section Momentum," UC Berkley, 2006.

Siegel, Jeremy J. *Stocks for the Long Run: A Definitive Guide to Financial Market Returns and Long-Term Investment Strategies*, New York: McGraw-Hill, 1994.

Taleb, Nassim N., *The Black Swan: The Impact of the Highly Improbable*. New York: Random House, 2007.

INDEX

A

account fees (mutual funds), 7
Accounting Review study of earnings estimates, 51
advancing stock market price-to-sales ratios, 78-81
Alpha Natural Gas (ANR), 126
analysts (security), market predictions, 50-53
ANR (Alpha Natural Gas), 126
anticipating changes, 20
averages (moving), adjusting for market capital risk with, 143-144

B

B (Barnes Group), 129
bargain model
    bargain list triggers, 120-122
    overview, 118
    price-to-sales ratio, 118
    relative price strength, 119
    reported earnings growth, 118
Barnes Group (B), 129
baskets of stocks, 12
behavior of markets, 20-21
Bennington, George, 66
Bogle, John
    on mutual fund fees, 8
    on mutual fund performance, 4
book value (net asset value), 58
borrowing on margin, 12
broker fees, 131
Brooks, Robert, 48
Burnham, Terry, 17
BusinessWeek magazine, study of economist forecasts, 48
buying stocks, 125-126, 154
buying long, 11

C

calculating data, 149
Capital Asset Pricing
   Model (CAPM), 28
capital risk variables, 113-116
CAPM (Capital Asset
   Pricing Model), 28
CF Industries (CF), 130
changes, anticipating, 20
charleskirkpatrick.com, 149
chartists, 42
charts, performance, 70-72
costs
   of execution, 131
   of research, 132

D

data services, 149
declining stock market
   price-to-sales ratios, 78-82
deleting stocks,
   127-130, 154-156
derivatives, 12
discipline, lack of, 25
distribution fees (mutual
   funds), 8
diversification, 30-31
drawdown, 32-33
   maximum, 138, 146
Dreman, David, 51

E

earnings
   earnings estimates, 51
   relative reporting earnings
      calculating, 86-87
      correlation with
         subsequent relative
         stock price
         performance, 87-92
      overview, 85
      summary, 93-94
economist market
   predictions, 47-49
efficient markets hypothesis
   (EMH), 42-46
emotions
   fear of being wrong, 23
   impatience, 23
   influence on market
      behavior, 20
   lack of discipline, 25
   perfectionism, 24
entry stops, 110
ETFs (Exchange Traded Funds)
evaluating markets, 21-22
exchange fees (mutual funds), 7
Exchange Traded Funds
   (ETFs), 13-14
expert market
   predictions, 49-50

Index

F
fear of being wrong, 23
fees, 131
  hedge fund fees, 13
  mutual fund fees, 7
Fidelity, 6
Filtered Waves, 66
finding data, 149
fundamental methods, 40-41
  versus technical methods, 39-40
funds
  ETFs (Exchange Traded Funds), 13-14
  hedge funds, 10-13
  mutual funds
    fees, 7
    market predictions, 50
    professional management of, 6-10

G
Gray, Brian, 48
growth model, 61-63
  bargain model, 118
  growth list triggers, 116-117
  overview, 109
  portfolio construction, 111-113
  stop orders, 110-111
  value list triggers, 117

H
hedge funds, 10-13
hedges, 11
hypothetical Value Model portfolios, 150-152

I
impatience, 23
Investment Act of 1940, 10
investment management
  hypothetical Value Model portfolios, 150-152
  overview, 3-4
  performance of Value Model, 152-153
  portfolios. *See* portfolios
  professional management
    ETFs (Exchange Traded Funds), 13-14
    hedge funds, 10-13
    mutual funds, 6-10
    past performance, 4-5
investment procedure
  adding and deleting stocks, 154-156
  finding and calculating data, 149
  hypothetical Value Model portfolios, 150-152
  performance of Value Model, 152-153
Investor Intelligence, Inc., 49
Investors' Business Daily, 95

J-K

Jegadeesh, Narisimhan, 96
Jensen, Michael, 66

Kirkpatrick Market Strategist (KMS), 133-135

L

lack of discipline, 25
law of percentages, 31
legislation, Investment Act of 1940, 10
leverage, 36
Levy, Robert A., 66
Lipper, Arthur, 66
liquidity, 36
liquidity squeeze, 36
Long Term Capital Management (LTCM), 43-46
looking for perfection, 24

M

management fees (mutual funds), 7
management of investments. *See* investment management
Mandel, Michael, 48
margin, 12
market capital risk, 33-37
    adjusting for using maximum number of stocks, 141-143
    adjusting for using simple moving averages, 143-144
market strategists, 49-50
markets
    behavior, 20-21
    evaluating, 21-22
    market capital risk, 33-37
        adjusting for using maximum number of stocks, 141-143
        adjusting for using simple moving averages, 143-144
    predictions
        compared to reactions, 53-55
        by economists, 47-49
        by experts, 49-50
        mutual funds, 50
        overview, 47
        by security analysts, 50-53
    reacting to, 53-55
maximum drawdown, 138, 146
maximum number of stocks, adjusting for market capital risk with, 141-143
Merrill, Arthur, 66
Motley Fool study of mutual fund performance, 4

Index

moving averages, adjusting for market capital risk with, 143-144
mutual funds
    fees, 7
    market predictions, 50
    professional management of, 6-10

N-O

net asset value (book value), 58
net worth, 58

O'Shaughnessy, James, 69

P

percentages, law of, 31
percentiles, 65
perfectionism, 24
performance
    correlation with relative reported earnings, 87-92
    performance charts, 70-72
    performance six months ahead, 74-76
    performance three months ahead, 73-74
    performance twelve months ahead, 77
    relative performance, 67-68
    of Value Model, 152-153
performance charts, 70-72

portfolios
    adding and deleting stocks, 154-156
    bargain model
        bargain list triggers, 120-122
        overview, 118
        price-to-sales ratio, 118
        relative price strength, 119
        reported earnings growth, 118
    creating, 133-138
        adjusting for risk using maximum number of stocks, 141-143
        adjusting for risk using simple moving averages, 143-144
        keeping fully invested, 139-141
        maximum drawdown, 146
        summary, 146-147
    growth model
        growth list triggers, 116-117
        overview, 109
        portfolio construction, 111-113
        stop orders, 111

managing, 133-135
value model
  capital risk
    variables, 113-116
  hypothetical value model
    portfolios, 150-152
  value list triggers, 117
predicting markets
  compared to reacting to
    markets, 53-55
  economists, 47-49
  experts, 49-50
  mutual funds, 50
  overview, 47
  security analysts, 50-53
price strength, 63-66
  bargain model, 119
  calculating, 95-105
  overview, 95, 105-107
price-to-earnings ratio, 59-60
price-to-sales ratio
  advancing and
    declining background
    market, 78-81
  advantages as measure
    of value, 69
  bargain model, 118
  declining background
    market, 81-82
  definition, 69
  performance six months
    ahead, 74-76
  performance three months
    ahead, 73-74
  performance twelve
    months ahead, 77
  summary, 83-84
prices
  price strength, 63-66
    bargain model, 119
    calculating, 95-105
    overview, 95, 105-107
  price-to-earnings
    ratio, 59-60
  price-to-sales ratio
    advancing and
      declining background
      market, 78-81
    advantages as measure
      of value, 69
    bargain model, 118
    declining background
      market, 81-82
    definition, 69
    performance six months
      ahead, 74-76
    performance three
      months ahead, 73-74
    performance twelve
      months ahead, 77
    summary, 83-84
  stop price, 110

Index

professional investment management
  ETFs (Exchange Traded Funds), 13-14
  hedge funds, 10-13
  mutual funds, 6-10
  past performance, 4-5
protective stops, 110
purchase fees (mutual funds), 7

Q-R

random walk, 29
randomness, 29-30
ratio method, 59-60
reacting to markets, 53-55
redemption fees (mutual funds), 7
relative data
  growth, 61-63
  overview, 57
  price strength, 63-66
    bargain model, 119
    calculating, 95-105
    overview, 95, 105-107
  price-to-sales ratio
    advancing and declining background market, 78-81
    advantages as measure of value, 69
    bargain model, 118
    declining background market, 81-82
    definition, 69
    performance six months ahead, 74-76
    performance three months ahead, 73-74
    performance twelve months ahead, 77
    summary, 83-84
  relative performance, 67-68
  relative reported earnings
    bargain model, 118
    calculating, 86-87
    correlation with subsequent relative stock price performance, 87-92
    overview, 85, 93-94
  sources of, 130-131
  value, 58-59
    net asset value (book value), 58
    net worth, 58
    ratio method, 59-60
reported earnings
  bargain model, 118
  calculating, 86-87
  correlation with subsequent relative stock price performance, 87-92
  overview, 85, 93-94

research, cost of, 132
risk, 17
    capital risk
        variables, 113-116
    defined, 27-29
    definition, 128
    diversification, 30-31
    drawdown, 32-33
    law of percentages, 31
    market capital risk
        adjusting for using maximum number of stocks, 141-143
        adjusting for using simple moving averages, 143-144
    market risk, 33-37
    maximum drawdown, 138
    randomness, 29
Ritholtz, Barry, 50
Royal Dutch/Shell, 43

S

sales loads (mutual funds), 7
security analyst market predictions, 50-53
selecting stocks, 125-126
selling stocks, 127-130, 154
    selling short, 11
setup, trigger, action (STRACT), 53-55
Sharpe Ratio, 28

Sharpe, William, 28
short squeeze, 11
Siegel, Jeremy, 15
sources of relative information, 130-131
standard deviation, 28
stocks
    adding, 154-156
    advantages of, 15-18
    Alpha Natural Gas (ANR), 126
    Barnes Group (B), 129
    baskets of stocks, 12
    buying, 125-126, 154
        buying long, 11
    CF Industries (CF), 130
    deleting, 127-130, 154-156
    derivatives, 12
    ETFs (Exchange Traded Funds), 13-14
    hedge funds, 10-13
    historical rate of return, 15-17
    mutual funds
        fees, 7
        market predictions, 50
        professional management of, 6-10
    relative data
        growth, 61-63
        overview, 57

Index

price strength, 63-66, 95-107
relative performance, 67-68
relative reported earnings, 85-92
sources of, 130-131
value. *See* value
risk, 17
selecting, 125-126
selling, 127-130, 154
selling short, 11
stop orders, 110-111
stop price, 110
STRACT (setup, trigger, action), 53-55

T

Technical Analysis: The Complete Reference for Financial Market Technicians, 2
technical analysts, 41
technical methods, 41-42
versus fundamental methods, 39-40
The Wall Street Journal study of economist forecasts, 48
Titman, Sheridan, 96
trailing stops, 110
12b-1 (distribution) fees, 8

U-Z

value, 58-59
net asset value (book value), 58
net worth, 58
performance charts, 70-72
price-to-sales ratio
advancing and declining background market, 78-81
advantages as measure of value, 69
declining background market, 81-82
definition, 69
performance six months ahead, 74-76
performance three months ahead, 73-74
performance twelve months ahead, 77
summary, 83-84
ratio method, 59-60
value model, 113-116
Value Line, 95
value model
hypothetical value model portfolios, 150-152
performance, 152-153

What Works on Wall Street, 69

FT Press
FINANCIAL TIMES

In an increasingly competitive world, it is quality of thinking that gives an edge—an idea that opens new doors, a technique that solves a problem, or an insight that simply helps make sense of it all.

We work with leading authors in the various arenas of business and finance to bring cutting-edge thinking and best-learning practices to a global market.

It is our goal to create world-class print publications and electronic products that give readers knowledge and understanding that can then be applied, whether studying or at work.

To find out more about our business products, you can visit us at www.ftpress.com.